SHORT WALKS

MAD

DO
WALKS
YORKSHIRE DALES

Ordnance Survey

Contents

Walk 1

RICHMOND AND EASBY

Distance
2.2miles/3.6km

Time
1¼ to 1¾ hrs

CATCH A BUS

Start/Finish
The Station, Richmond

Parking DL10 4LD
The Station car park

Cafés/pubs
The Station Café; The Easby Loop Café; The King's Head Hotel

Drummer boy legend; old railway line to Easby Abbey; River Swale return

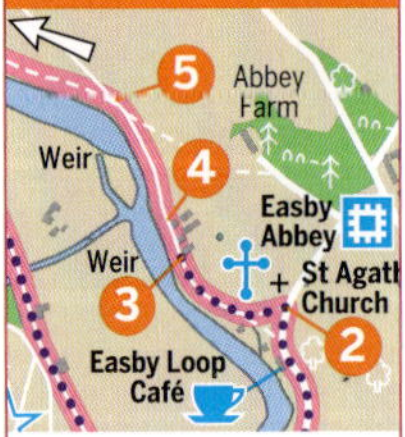

Page 14

Walk 2

CASTLE BOLTON AND REDMIRE

Distance
2.8 miles/4.5km

Time
1¾ to 2¼ hrs

CATCH A BUS

Start/Finish
Castle Bolton

Parking DL8 4ET
Bolton Castle car park

Cafés/pubs
Wensleydale Tea Rooms, Bolton Castle; Redmire Village Pub

Impressive castle; charming Wensleydale villages; the 'White Lady'

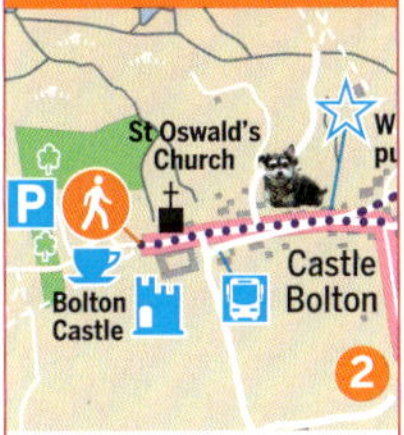

Page 20

Walk 3

BAINBRIDGE

Distance
2.2 miles/3.5km

Time
1¼ to 1¾ hrs

CATCH A BUS

Start/Finish
Bainbridge village green

Parking DL8 3EL
Roadside parking around the village green

Cafés/pubs
A Taste of Wensleydale Bakery and Tea Room; Rose & Crown Hotel

Horn-blower tradition; England's shortest river; Roman fort; hydro power

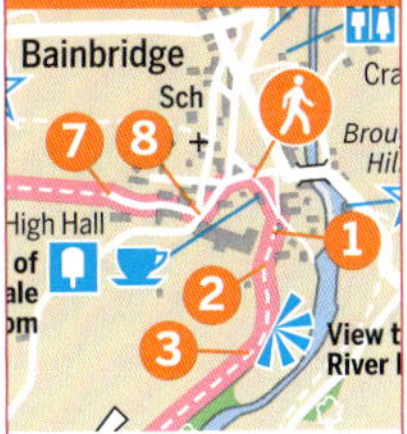

Page 28

Walk 4

HAWES, HARDRAW AND SEDBUSK

Distance
4.1 miles/6.6km

Time
2¼ to 2¾ hrs

CATCH A BUS

Start/Finish
Hawes

Parking DL8 3NT
National Park car park, Hawes

Cafés/pubs
Firebox Café; White Hart Inn; Green Dragon

Dark Skies Festival; Dales museum; mighty waterfall; cheese delight

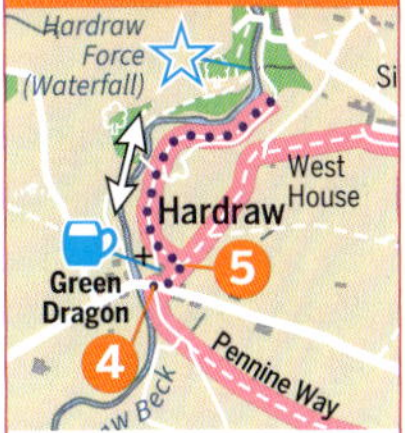

Page 34

Walk 5

KETTLEWELL TO BUCKDEN

Distance
4.4 miles/7km

Time
2½ to 3 hrs

CATCH A BUS

Start Kettlewell

Finish Buckden

Parking BD23 5QZ
National Park car park, Kettlewell

Cafés/pubs
Kettlewell; Starbotton; Buckden

Dales Way walk beside the River Wharfe; lead mining; *Calendar Girls*

Page 42

Walk 6

CLAPHAM AND INGLEBOROUGH CAVE

Distance
3.2 miles/5.1km

Time
1¾ to 2¼ hrs

CATCH A BUS

Start/Finish
Clapham

Parking LA2 8EA
National Park car park, Clapham

Cafés/pubs
The Old Sawmill Café; The Old Manor House; picnic benches

Wonder cave; Aunt Bessie's Grotto; Thwaite Scars; beware the boggart!

Page 48

Walk 7

SETTLE AND GIGGLESWICK

Distance
2.2 miles/3.6km

Time
1¼ to 1¾ hrs

GO BY TRAIN
CATCH A BUS

Start/Finish
Kirkgate, Settle

Parking BD24 9DZ
Ashfield car park, Kirkgate

Cafés/pubs
The Wonky Cake Café; The Golden Lion; Settle

Flowerpot Festival; world's oldest music hall; Queen's Rock

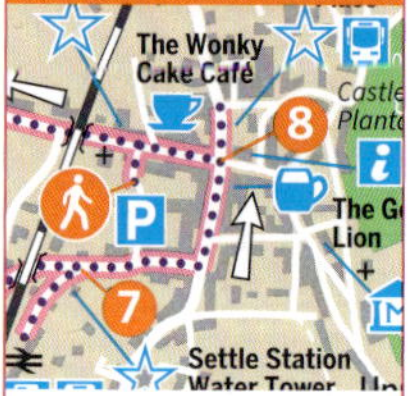

Page 54

Walk 8

GRIMWITH RESERVOIR

Distance
4.3 miles/7km

Time
2½ to 3 hrs

Start/Finish
Grimwith Reservoir

Parking BD23 5ED
Yorkshire Water's Grimwith Reservoir car park

Cafés/pubs
Seasonal ice cream van; Time Café, Stump Cross Cavern

A reservoir circuit in a Dales moorland setting; sailing; bird watching

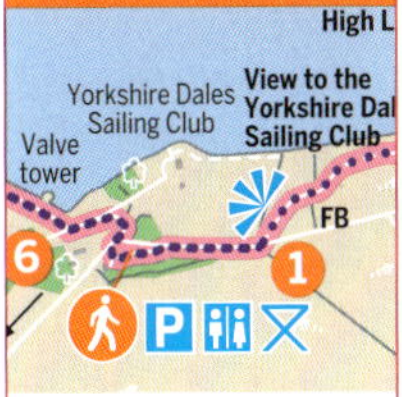

Page 62

Walk 9

BURNSALL

Distance
2.5 miles/4km

Time
1½ to 2 hrs

CATCH A BUS

Start/Finish
Burnsall

Parking BD23 6BS
Burnsall car park

Cafés/pubs
River bank Café; Wharfe View Tea Room; Red Lion Hotel

Charming Dales village; superb scenery; historic bridge and church

Page 68

Walk 10

SKIPTON CASTLE WOODS

Distance
1.9 miles/3.1km

Time
1¼ to 1¾ hrs

GO BY TRAIN
CATCH A BUS

Start/Finish
The Bailey, Skipton

Parking BD23 1UA
The Bailey car park

Cafés/pubs
Kibble Bakery Coffee House; The Castle Inn

Delightful woodland walk beside Eller Beck; castle; town hall museum

Page 74

GETTING OUTSIDE IN THE YORKSHIRE DALES WITH YOUR DOG

Ted at Clapham

“”

Walks guide you to two of Yorkshire's great natural wonders – Hardraw Force and Ingleborough Cave

OS Champion Emily Gill

A very warm welcome to the Short Walks Made Easy guide to dog-friendly walks in the Yorkshire Dales – a fantastic selection of leisurely routes perfect for you and your pooch!

The Yorkshire Dales is a wonderful location for walking with your dog. Here's a great selection of dales, becks, charming villages and dog-friendly places, pubs and cafés to make the most of your stay.

All ten dog-friendly routes are relaxing and enjoyable, with or without a canine companion, but to make the most of each walk for your dog, we highlight safe water entry points, sources of drinking water and scenic rest stops. In the walk information panel you'll find where dogs must be kept on leads and where off-lead running is possible. These are all family-friendly excursions and a great way for walkers of all ages and abilities to explore the Yorkshire Dales with their four-legged friend.

You can stroll peacefully in Wensleydale at Hawes, Bainbridge and Redmire, and in Wharfedale at Kettlewell, Buckden and Burnsall. Walks guide you to two of Yorkshire's great natural wonders – Hardraw Force and Ingleborough Cave; visit historic strongholds in Richmond, Castle Bolton and Skipton; and take post-walk refreshment in the charming village tea rooms and pubs in Burnsall, Settle and Starbotton. Take in moorland scenery at Grimwith Reservoir, see the world's oldest music hall in Settle, stargaze at Dark Skies sites, and enjoy the spooky stories across the Dales, including the drummer boy, the White Lady and the mischievous boggarts.

Emily Gill,
OS Champion

WE ARE HAPPIEST WHEN WE'RE OUT WITH OUR DOGS

"No matter how bad my day was, a simple dog walk makes everything better"

Ted's CV

- **What breed is he?** Patterjack
- **How old is he?** Nine
- **Favourite walk?** scent-rich tracks and exploring the edges of drystone walls

Ted on the Kettlewell to Buckden walk

Whether it's a stroll before breakfast or a weekend wander through the woods, we know that getting outside with your dog is one of life's pleasures. A wagging tail, fresh air and a good walk. What more could you ask for?

At Ordnance Survey (OS), we're passionate about helping people and their four-legged friends explore the outdoors with confidence. Through our trusted mapping, guides and digital tools, we aim to make dog walking easy, enjoyable and accessible, so you and your dogs can live well, stay active and discover new adventures together.

We believe the outdoors is for everyone and for every dog: from coastal paths perfect for a paddle, to shady woodland trails and open countryside where dogs can enjoy some time off-lead. Great Britain is packed with incredible places to explore. Our dog-friendly walking series is full of inspiration, with handpicked routes that are safe, scenic and suitable for all kinds of dogs and their human families.

We know that heading out with your dog can come with its own set of questions: whether there's livestock nearby, how many tricky stiles, or if there's a stream for a splash. That's why we've teamed up with experienced authors who all own dogs.

If you're looking for fresh ideas or easy-to-follow walks in a new location, we hope this series inspires you to spend more time outside with your canine companion. We'll be with you every step (and pawprint) of the way.

To find out more visit os.uk/discover

RESPECTING THE COUNTRYSIDE

You can't beat getting outside in the British countryside, but it's vital that we leave no trace when we're enjoying the great outdoors.

Let's make sure that generations to come can enjoy the countryside just as we do.

- Leave no trace
- Keep dogs under control; bag and bin waste
- Do not light fires; only BBQ at official sites
- Leave gates as you find them
- Keep to footpaths and open access land
- Plan ahead for your trip

For more details please visit gov.uk/countryside-code

USING THIS GUIDE

Easy-to-follow dog-friendly walks in the Yorkshire Dales

Before setting off

Check the walk information panel to plan your outing

- The suggested **Time** is based on a gentle pace and allows additional off-lead roaming and playtime for your dog
- Consider using **Public transport** where flagged. If driving, note the satnav postcode for the car park under **Parking**
- Note the availability of **Cafés**, tearooms and pubs, and **Toilets**

Terrain and hilliness

- **Terrain** indicates the nature of the route surface
- Any rises and falls are noted under **Hilliness**

Footwear and accessibility

- Check the advice under **Footwear** for deciding whether to wear shoes or boots
- **Accessibility** indicates the parts of the walk that should be suitable for wheelchairs and pushchairs

A perfectly pocket-sized walking guide

- Handily sized for ease of use on each walk
- When not being read, it fits nicely into a pocket...
- ...so between points, put this book in the pocket of your coat, trousers or day sack and enjoy your stroll in glorious countryside – we've made it pocket-sized for a reason!

Flexibility of route presentation to suit all readers

- **Not comfortable map reading?** Then use the simple-to-follow route profile and accompanying route description and pictures
- **Happy to map read?** New-look walk mapping makes it easier for you to focus on the route and the points of interest along the way
- **Read the insightful Did you know?, Local legend, Stories behind the walk** and **Nature notes** to help you make the most of your day out and to enjoy all that each walk has to offer

OS information about the walk

- Many of the features and symbols shown are taken from Ordnance Survey's celebrated **Explorer** mapping, designed to help people across Great Britain enjoy leisure time spent outside

- National Grid reference for the start point
- Explorer sheet map covering the route

OS information
NZ 177008
Explorer 304

The easy-to-use walk map

- **Large-scale** mapping for ultra-clear route finding

- **Numbered points** at key turns along the route that tie in with the route instructions and respective points marked on the profile

- **Pictorial symbols** for intuitive map reading, see Map Symbols on the front cover flap

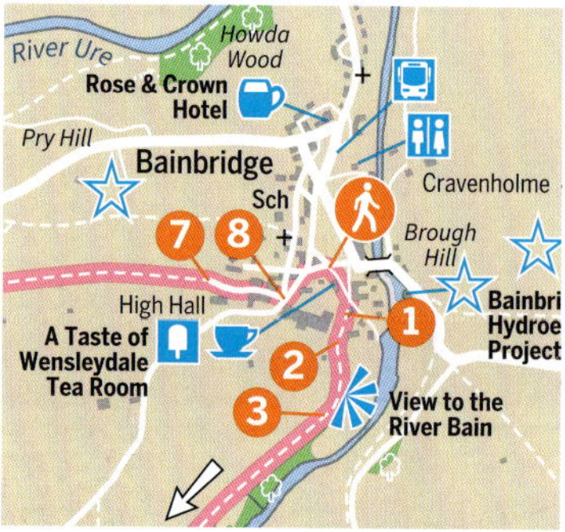

The simple-to-follow walk profile

- Progress easily along the route using the illustrative profile, it has **numbered points** for key turning points and **graduated distance** markers

- Easy-read **route directions** with turn-by-turn detail

- Reassuring **route photographs** for each numbered point

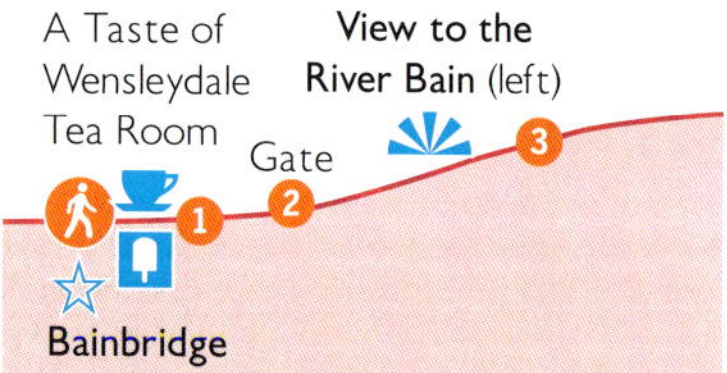

2 ➡ Pass through the gate and steadily climb the track into wooded pastureland. There are views of the river to your left.

Using QR codes

- Scan each QR code to see the route in Ordnance Survey's OS Maps App
NB You may need to download a scanning app if you have an older phone

- OS Maps will open the route automatically if you have it installed. If not, the route will open in the web version of OS Maps

- Please click **Start Route** button to begin navigating or **Download Route** to store the route for offline use

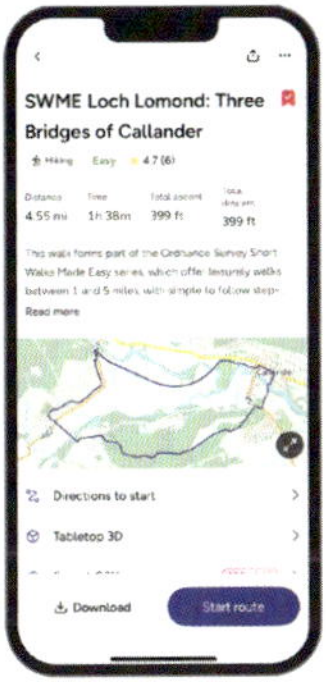

Ted's tips

- Know where your dog must be **on a lead**, where there is likely to be livestock and (seasonally) ground-nesting birds, and where your dog can have **off-lead time**

- Check the number of **stiles** and where your dog may need lifting, and any awkward gates and flights of steps

- Safe water entry points and sources of **drinking water** for your dog (see the Ted icon on the maps and profiles)

- Note any shared-use paths

WALK 1

RICHMOND AND EASBY

Setting out from the charming town of Richmond, this beautiful circular walk combines history, nature and dog-friendly fun. Starting from The Station, the route follows the tranquil, tree-lined old railway line to Easby Abbey, and returns on a leafy riverside path beside the Swale – perfect for paddling, wildlife spotting and pausing to enjoy the scenery, just like Ted does! Richmond Castle and the picturesque Market Place is a ten-minute stroll from The Station car park.

OS information

NZ 177008
Explorer 304

Distance
2.2 miles/3.6km

Time
1¼ to 1¾ hours

Start/Finish
The Station, Richmond

Parking DL10 4LD
The Station car park (pay and display), just south of the River Swale off the A6136

Public toilets
Richmond: The Falls, Riverside Road, DL10 4JR; Nuns Close, Hurgill Road, DL10 4UN

Cafés/pubs
The Station Café at start; The Easby Loop Café near 2; in Richmond, The King's Head Hotel

Terrain
Firm old railway path; surfaced paths and pavement; grassy tracks, woodland paths; rough lane

Hilliness
Generally flat with one short climb after 6

Footwear
Year round in dry conditions; after wet weather

Did you know? Richmond's expansive cobbled Market Place is among the largest in England, and beneath it lies a network of medieval vaults and cellars, some of which are still in use today by local businesses and traders.

Local legend In the 18th century, there was a myth that Richmond Castle and Easby Abbey were linked by a secret tunnel. According to legend, a drummer boy ventured into the tunnel beneath the castle's keep, beating his drum to signal his progress. As the locals followed above ground, the steady rhythm suddenly stopped near Easby Abbey, and the boy vanished without a trace. Some say you can still hear his ghostly drumming, a chilling reminder of his mysterious fate.

Public transport

Bus services X26/X27, between Darlington and Catterick, to the stop at 🚶: arrivabus.co.uk

Accessibility

Powered wheelchairs from 🚶 to 3, with return by the outward route. All-terrain wheelchair loan available from Richmond Swimming Pool. All-terrain pushchairs throughout, but with a stile at 3, and steps after 5

Ted's tips

Off-lead walking along the old railway line 🚶 to 1 but look out for cyclists on the shared-use path. Keep on leads in fields where there are livestock on the return. One small, wooden stile at 3

STORIES BEHIND THE WALK

☆ The Eryholme–Richmond branch line

The disused railway path was once part of the Eryholme–Richmond branch line, opened in 1846 by the York and Newcastle Railway. It connected Richmond to the national network, supporting local trade and military transport, especially to Catterick Garrison. Famous for its impressive Victorian station, the line was closed in 1969 under the Beeching cuts. In 1974, the site was repurposed as a garden centre, which closed in 2001. The building was restored and reopened as The Station in 2007.

Easby Abbey

Founded in 1152 by Roald, constable of Richmond Castle, Easby Abbey was a Premonstratensian monastery beside the River Swale. Known for its peaceful setting and beautiful Gothic architecture, it became a wealthy religious community. Henry VIII disbanded the abbey in 1536 during the Dissolution of the Monasteries. Today, its well-preserved ruins, including the refectory and gatehouse, offer a glimpse into medieval monastic life.

½ mile

☆ The Eryholme branc

The Station car park

➡ From the bottom end of the car park, having passed The Station (right) and Richmond Swimming Pool (left), keep **ahead** along the old railway path, signed Easby.

➡ Walk to a broad bridge over the River Swale in ¾ mile.

1 ➡ Immediately after crossing the bridge, turn **left**, signed Easby, along a track (Love Lane).

➡ The river is now on your left. Bend **left** on the riverside path to The Easby Loop Café.

➡ Keep **ahead** to St Agatha's Church and monastic ruins.

2 ➡ After visiting the abbey site, turn **right** out of the church gate and follow the surfaced path to its end at a metal vehicle gate and small wooden stile.

Richmond Castle

Construction of Richmond Castle began in 1071 following the Norman Conquest and this striking fortress played a pivotal role in securing the region for William the Conqueror. Its towering 12th-century keep remains a dominant feature of the landscape. Over the centuries, the castle evolved from a military stronghold to a noble residence and later served as a prison during World War I. From the top, the castle provides panoramic views over the town.

☆ Richmond

Richmond is one of the most complete historic market towns in England. Its prominent cobbled Market Place, one of the largest in the country, has been hosting weekly markets since receiving its royal charter from King Henry II in 1155. The Georgian Theatre Royal, built in 1788, is one of the oldest working theatres still in its original form. The town is also home to a rare 18th-century obelisk and features an elegant range of Georgian and Victorian architecture.

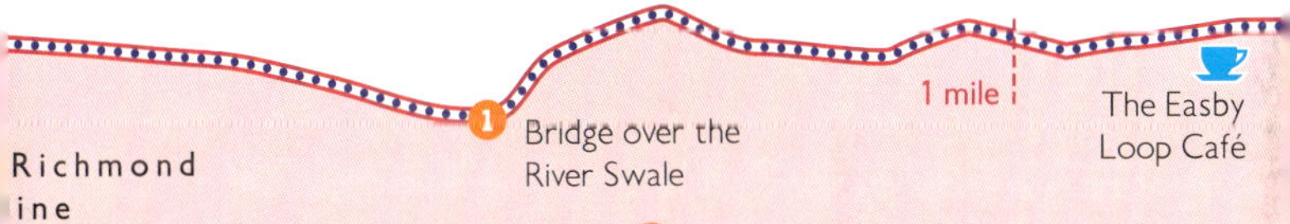

3 ➡ The public footpath is well signposted. Go over the stile and walk across a gravelled drive, passing a house (right).
➡ In the corner you will see a footpath sign, leading to a small track. Proceed along it for a few yards to a gate.

4 ➡ Pass through the gate onto a well-trodden track across open grassland beside the river. Look out for the conservation area plaque (left).
➡ Follow the track, river on the left, bearing **left** to a path junction and kissing-gate.

NATURE NOTES

A canopy of oak, ash and sycamore makes the disused railway line a pleasant path to walk in summer, while along the verges, red campion, yarrow and knapweed flourish. The meadows around Easby Abbey are vibrant with blooming cowslips, in spring, and oxeye daisies and buttercups in early summer. Across the abbey's grassy cloisters, valerian grows on the crumbling stone walls. Wetland flowers such as purple loosestrife, meadowsweet and yellow flag iris can be seen along the banks of the River Swale.

The holly blue is an interesting hedgerow butterfly that has two broods a year: females in the spring brood lay their eggs on holly, after which the species is named, whereas ivy is targeted in the second, late-summer brood. The damper grassy areas near the River Swale and verges along the old railway line that receive dappled sunlight attract ringlet butterflies. In the grassland of the open meadows, you are more likely to spot meadow browns.

Ringlet

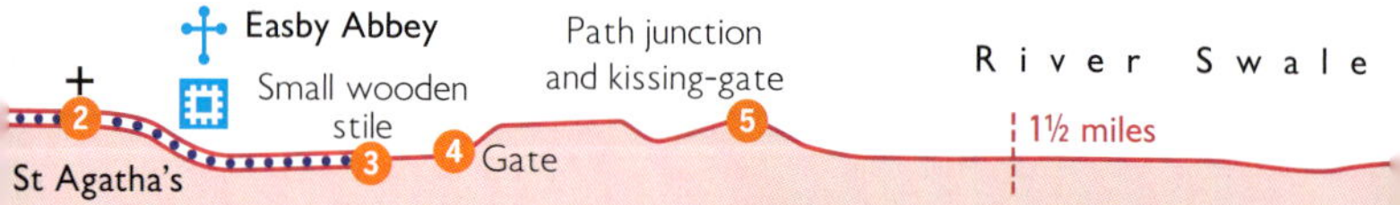

5 ➡ Here the path splits. This walk follows the riverside way, but to avoid descending a set of steps, the higher path also leads to **6**.

➡ Go through the gate to follow the lower-level route.

➡ Descend stone steps and pick up a wide woodland track. It soon narrows and becomes a surfaced pathway, later widening to a lane.

➡ Pass a small rock face covered with mosses and lichens to reach a roughly surfaced lane, where the upper and lower paths meet.

Above: holly blue
Below: common frog; conservation area

Top: cowslips
Bottom: sycamore samaras

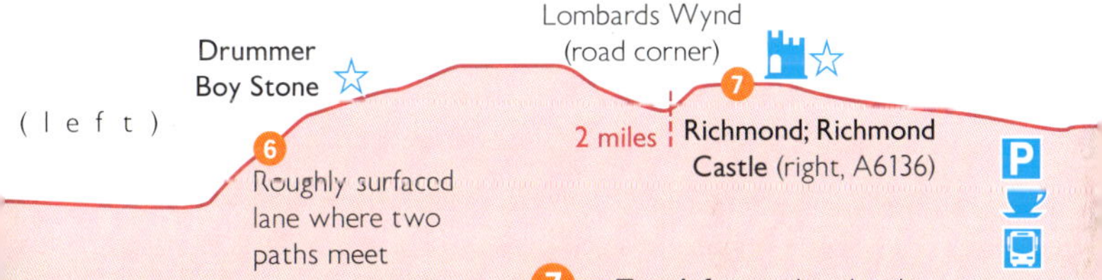

6 ➨ At the junction, on the right, is the Drummer Boy Stone.
➨ Keep **ahead** and follow the lane for ¼ mile, passing a row of cottages (left) near the end and soon coming to a junction at a road corner.

7 ➨ Turn **left** onto Lombards Wynd and walk to the main road.
➨ You can turn **right** here and follow the pavement into the town centre.
➨ Or you can turn **left** onto the bridge and walk back to The Station car park.

CATCH A BUS

WALK 2

CASTLE BOLTON AND REDMIRE

Bolton Castle, once a stronghold of medieval power, still dominates the Wensleydale landscape. This gentle walk to Redmire, rich in heritage and full of charm, follows old field paths and quiet lanes that were once travelled by castle stewards. It is an ideal route for dogs, offering plenty of space to roam and streamside spots for cooling off. Ted's favourite moment? Sitting peacefully on the bench overlooking the castle, with his tail wagging as walkers passed by.

OS information

SE 032918
Explorer OL30

Distance
2.8 miles/4.5km

Time
1¾ to 2¼ hours

Start/Finish
Castle Bolton

Parking DL8 4ET
Bolton Castle car park (pay and display)

Public toilets
In the car park and within Bolton Castle grounds

Cafés/pubs
Wensleydale Tea Rooms at Bolton Castle; Redmire Village Pub

Terrain
Lanes; grassy tracks; field and surfaced paths

Hilliness
Gently undulating

Footwear
Year round ; in dry conditions

Public transport
Bus services 156, between Leyburn and Gayle, to the Castle stop, Castle Bolton, and Monument stop, Redmire: littlewhitebus.co.uk; and 857, summer Sundays only, between Garsdale Station and Redmire: dalesbus.org

Accessibility

The route is not accessible due to narrow gates. Pushchairs will need lifting to avoid the narrow gates and gaps. However, a longer route to Redmire from Bolton Castle is possible via quiet East Lane, then turning right onto Hargill Lane to reach Redmire.

Ted's tips

Welcome but keep on a lead in the fields (livestock). No stiles, but narrow gates and gaps. At Bolton Castle, dogs are not permitted in the castle, garden and main tea room, but an outdoor seated area is provided; the Redmire Village Pub is dog friendly

Did you know? Bolton Castle has long been a popular location for filmmakers due to its authentic medieval architecture and striking scenery. It has appeared in productions such as *Ivanhoe*, *Elizabeth*, *Anne Boleyn*, *Heartbeat*, and *All Creatures Great and Small*. The castle's well-preserved interiors and towering walls provide a stunning backdrop for historical dramas, making it one of Yorkshire's best historic filming locations.

Local legend Bolton Castle has a reputation for being one of the most haunted locations in Yorkshire. Its best-known spirit, the 'White Lady', is believed to be either Mary, Queen of Scots, or a sorrowful ancestor of the Scrope family. Visitors frequently report seeing a veiled woman drifting through the ruins, often accompanied by sudden chills and the unexplained sound of footsteps.

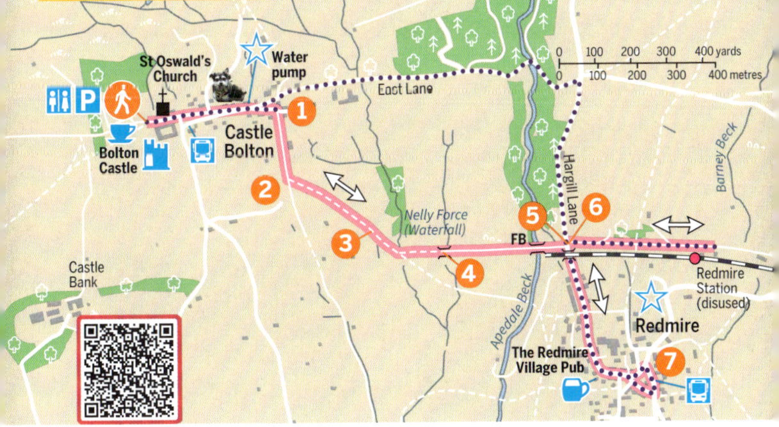

STORIES BEHIND THE WALK

Bolton Castle Constructed between 1378 and 1399 by Sir Richard le Scrope, Bolton Castle is one of the best-preserved medieval fortresses in England. The castle's imposing walls, keep and original features offer insight into medieval life and the strategic defence of Wensleydale. Notably, it was where Mary, Queen of Scots, was held captive from 1568 to 1569. Designed to serve both as a residence and a stronghold, it played a crucial role for the Royalists during the English Civil War (boltoncastle.co.uk).

St Oswald's Church A hidden gem, St Oswald's Church was built around the same time as Bolton Castle. The church embodies the simple Gothic style characteristic of rural churches. One notable feature is the low-side lancet window, also known as a leper window. This narrow opening allowed those affected by leprosy to observe services from outside. Additionally, during her imprisonment at Bolton Castle, Mary, Queen of Scots, is said to have worshipped here.

Dog drinking water barrel

Water pump (left)

Rough drive; signpost to Redmire Station

Village green

St Oswald's Church (left)

Bolton Castle (right)

Bolton Castle car park

Drystone wall gap (left)

½ mile

Bench and old stone building (left)

Gated and stepped bridge

➡ From the car park, follow the lane past the castle (right) and church (left) and keep **ahead** along the top of the green.

➡ Fork **right** towards the end of the green, **cross** the village lane and bear **right** on a rough drive, walking to a sign for Redmire Station.

1 ➡ Turn **right** at the signpost and follow a grassy track, passing through a metal farm gate.

➡ Continue past farm buildings then go through a wide gap.

➡ Keep **ahead** along the left-hand field edge until you reach a gap in the drystone wall in 70 yards.

☆ Water pump

Nestled beside a wall on the village green, the old iron water pump stands beside a stone trough. Once vital for daily life, it provided water for both villagers and livestock before the mains supply arrived. Although no longer in use, its tap and signage remain, quietly echoing a time of shared community life, preserved as part of the village's heritage.

☆ Redmire

A small village with medieval origins, Redmire is known for its traditional stone cottages and historic green. The village developed around farming and local stone quarrying, with distinctive roofing slate supplied to the surrounding area. Redmire's green was once the focus of livestock fairs and village gatherings, reflecting its agricultural roots. Many of the cottages date back to the 17th and 18th centuries. Redmire Station was the western terminus of the Wensleydale Railway, currently undergoing restoration (wensleydale-railway.co.uk/stations-redmire).

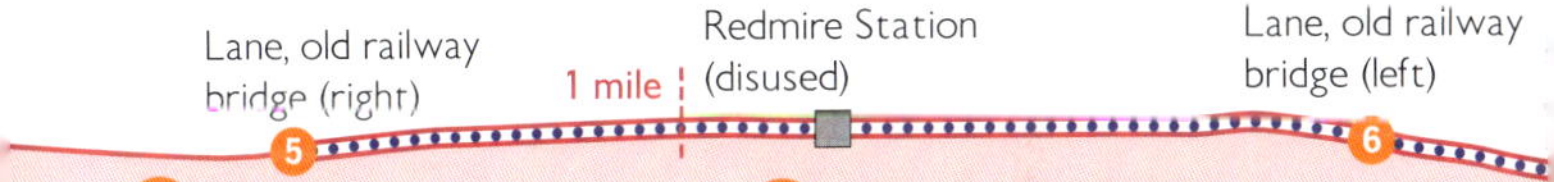

2 ➡ Turn **left**, through the gap and follow the well-trodden path across the field and pass through a gate.
➡ Maintain your direction across the next field to a further gate. Go through and enter a small area of scrub, with a bench and old stone building (left).

3 ➡ The path widens and descends towards trees.
➡ Follow the path through the trees, soon crossing a small bridge.
➡ Continue to the next bridge, which is much larger, and has a small wooden gate in front of it and two steps at each side.

NATURE NOTES

Buzzards circle on the thermals above farmland and the tree-lined field edges, their mewing calls often heard near the castle grounds. Kestrels hover over rough pasture and roadside verges, hunting for small mammals.

Belts of broadleaved woodland line the lanes, bridleways and footpaths, field boundaries and riverbanks between Castle Bolton and Redmire, and comprise English (or pedunculate) oak, ash and sycamore, the leaves of which turn rich yellows and bronzes in autumn. These woodland strips are most noticeable along the Apedale Beck, looking down from the old railway bridge.

Wildflowers thrive in the meadows, field margins and verges, adding vibrant colour to the landscape. The meadows near Redmire feature yellow rattle, knapweed and orchids, all of which are vital for pollinators. Hedgerows and drystone walls provide shelter for wild violets and red campion.

Within the grounds of the castle, roe deer are sometimes observed moving quietly near the ancient stonework, particularly at dawn and dusk.

Violets

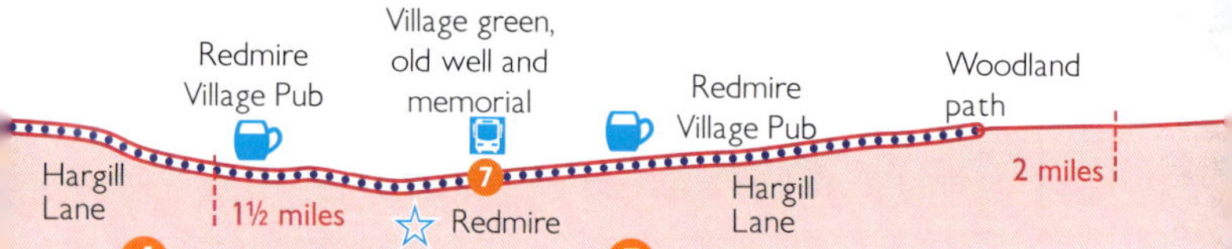

4 ➨ Go through the gate and cross the bridge. The ongoing track winds through the woodland towards Redmire, soon reaching a lane. A former railway bridge can be seen to the right.

5 ➨ **Cross** the lane and bear slightly **left** for the lane leading to Redmire Station, which is currently disused, but worth the detour (400 yards each way) to see it. ➨ Return to the lane.

Roe deer

Left: acorns and oak leaves
Middle: ash buds
Right: sycamore leaves

Water pump (right)

Dog drinking water barrel

Village green

St Oswald's Church (right)

2½ miles

Bolton Castle (left)

Bolton Castle car park

6 ➡ Go **left** and pass under the old railway bridge, heading along Hargill Lane towards Redmire.

➡ Entering the village, the pub is on the corner to your right and straight ahead is the pretty village green, with its old well and memorial.

7 ➡ After exploring the village, return past the Redmire Village Pub along Hargill Lane.

➡ After passing under the old railway bridge, turn **left** on the woodland path and retrace your outward steps back to Castle Bolton.

This page (clockwise): Bainbridge; Hardraw to Hawes fingerpost; Richmond Castle
Opposite page (clockwise): Castle Bolton; Settle; Upper Wharfedale; Grimwith Reservoir

National Trust
Upper Wharfedale
Welcome

WALK 3

CATCH A BUS

BAINBRIDGE

Starting from the picturesque village green, this well-marked route leads through open fields, ancient earthworks and stretches of Roman road, with sweeping views across Wensleydale. Gates and clear signage make navigation easy. Ted loves the scent-rich tracks, watching rabbits, and exploring the edges of drystone walls. It is a peaceful and varied walk that combines heritage, scenery and plenty of dog-friendly interest along the way.

OS information

SD 933900
Explorer OL30

Distance
2.2 miles/3.5km

Time
1¼ to 1¾ hours

Start/Finish
Bainbridge village green

Parking DL8 3EL
Roadside parking, with consideration, around the village green

Public toilets
By the recreation ground on the village green

Cafés/pubs
A Taste of Wensleydale Bakery and Tea Room; Rose & Crown Hotel

Terrain
Lanes; field paths and tracks

Hilliness
Moderate ascent from start to 4 and descent from 4 to end

Footwear
Spring/summer/ Autumn, Winter

Public transport
Bus service 156, between Leyburn and Gayle, to the stop at the northern end of the green: littlewhitebus.co.uk

Accessibility
Not suitable for wheelchairs, other than around the village green; all-terrain pushchairs in dry conditions

Ted's tips
Keep on a lead in the village and in fields with livestock. One stile and some narrow gates

Did you know? Bainbridge had an ancient horn-blowing custom that was maintained until late into the 20th century. Every evening from late September until Shrove Tuesday, the horn would be blown. The first documented source of this tradition is from the 1820s, but its origins are believed to be much older. In medieval times, Bainbridge was the administrative centre of the Forest of Wensleydale and the horn may have been blown as a guide to travellers.

Local legend Semer Water lies 1½ miles south of Bainbridge. According to legend, a lost town lies buried beneath its surface, a once-thriving community that was swept away by a mysterious flood. The story goes that only one family showed kindness to a wandering stranger, while the rest turned him away. In revenge, the stranger unleashed a torrent of water, which engulfed the town and created the lake. On still evenings, you may hear the faint sound of church bells echoing from the sunken ruins.

Scan Me

STORIES BEHIND THE WALK

☆ **Virosidum Roman Fort** Located on Brough Hill, immediately east of the village, the fort overlooks the River Bain and the River Ure. It was built between 90 and 105 CE, originally featuring timber defences that were later replaced with stone. The site was occupied until the late fourth century. Excavations conducted between the 1920s and 1960s established it was a significant military stronghold, finding inscriptions associated with the Sixth Cohort of Nerviorum.

☆ **Bainbridge** The name 'Bainbridge' has Old Norse and Old English roots. 'Bain' derives from the Norse word 'beinn', meaning straight or direct, referencing the River Bain's straight course. 'Bridge' is from the Old English 'brycg', denoting a crossing point. In combination the name highlights Bainbridge's importance as a direct and convenient river crossing in Wensleydale, essential to early travel and settlement in the Yorkshire Dales.

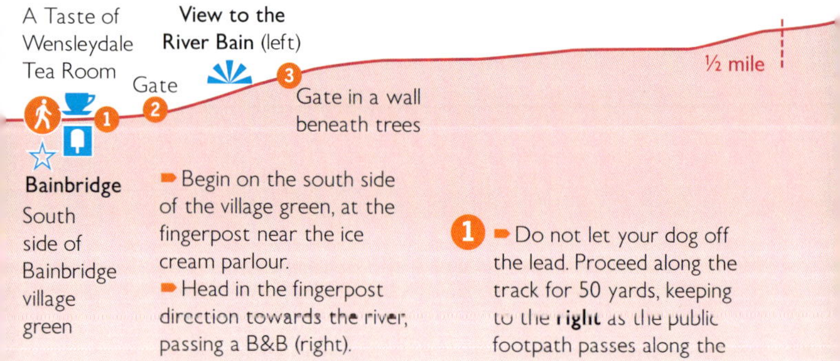

Bainbridge
South side of Bainbridge village green

➡ Begin on the south side of the village green, at the fingerpost near the ice cream parlour.
➡ Head in the fingerpost direction towards the river, passing a B&B (right).
➡ Immediately after, bear **right** on a grassy lane running between cottages.

1 ➡ Do not let your dog off the lead. Proceed along the track for 50 yards, keeping to the **right** as the public footpath passes along the driveway through the garden of a private residence and up a couple of steps to a gate.

☆ Bainbridge Hydroelectric Project

The community-owned archimedes-screw hydroelectric installation was opened in May 2011. It uses the River Bain's 10-foot drop to generate up to 45kw of power, which is sufficient to supply around 40 homes, although recent dry summers have reduced output. It is hoped to save over 3,000 tons of CO^2 over its 40-year lifespan.

☆ River Bain

The River Bain is often quoted as being the shortest named river in England. Measuring just 2½ miles long, it flows gently from its source at Semer Water to its confluence with the River Ure, just north of Bainbridge. Over its course, the Bain drops about 150 feet, passing through Dales farmland and then to the eastern side of the village on its way to join the Ure.

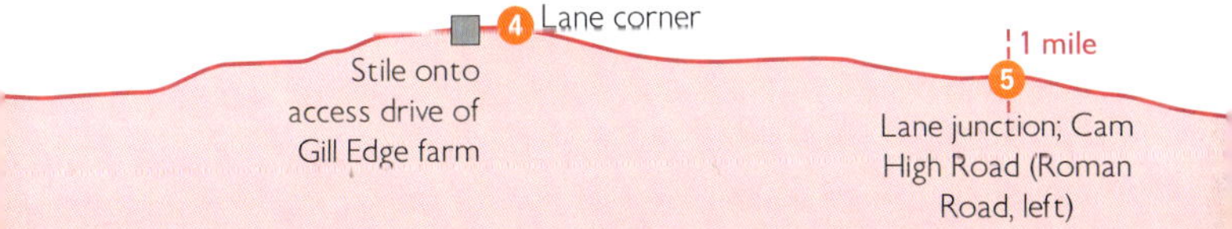

2 ➨ Pass through the gate and steadily climb the track into wooded pastureland. There are views of the river to your left.

➨ Follow the well-trodden path to a gate in a wall beneath trees.

3 ➨ Go through the gate. Continue to follow the clear path from field to field, passing through waymarked gates.

➨ After just over ½ mile, reach Gill Edge farm. Turn **right** over a stile along the farm access track to a lane corner.

NATURE NOTES

The fast-moving waters of the River Bain are home to brown trout, best seen near the old stepping stones, and downstream towards the weir. Water voles can sometimes be spotted along the quieter, reedy banks, while otters may occasionally be glimpsed at dawn or dusk near the river's bends, taking advantage of the rich aquatic life.

Roe deer often graze quietly on the edges of nearby woodlands and meadows, their tawny coats blending with the landscape. Rabbits are plentiful in the fields and hedgerows around the village, where they create burrow networks.

Swallows return annually from southern Africa in spring, nesting in barns and outbuildings, and feeding exclusively on insects caught mid-air, a common sight above the riverbanks and Bainbridge's fields.

In summer, the meadows, riverbanks and path verges come alive with insects. Look out for colourful butterflies, including small copper, meadow brown, peacock and small tortoiseshell, flitting among the wildflowers.

Swallow

5 ➨ Go through the metal gate, the fingerpost directing you across a small enclosure to a further fingerpost and wooden gate.
➨ Pass through the gate and follow the grassy track diagonally **left** as it sweeps down the valley, going through a gate at the bottom towards the buildings at Greensley Bank.

4 ➨ Turn **right** onto the lane and follow it for ¼ mile to a metal field gate and fingerpost on the **left** at a lane junction. (Cam High Road, a Roman road, joins the lane here from the left.)

Top left: water vole
Above: small copper
Bottom left: rabbit
Below: meadow brown

Gate into a car park on the edge of Bainbridge

The main village road

2 miles

Bainbridge

South side of Bainbridge village green

6 ➨ Approaching the buildings, turn **right** through a gateway, passing them on your right.
➨ Carry on along the path for ¾ mile, across a succession of fields with intermediate gates, to a gate on the edge of Bainbridge.

7 ➨ Go through the gate and walk through a car park belonging to the Yorkshire Dales National Park office.
➨ Keep **ahead** along the access road through a residential area to a T-junction with the village road.

8 ➨ Turn **left** onto the village road. Watching out for approaching traffic, walk through the village, turning **right** (Aysgarth and Leyburn direction) to return to the south side of the green.

WALK 4

CATCH A BUS

HAWES, HARDRAW AND SEDBUSK

This circuit from Hawes offers stunning views of Wensleydale, peaceful lanes, riverside paths, and an opportunity to visit Hardraw Force. It is perfect for dog walkers, featuring plenty of off-lead sections in the fields, shaded paths and places for splashing about. The varied terrain keeps the walk engaging without being overly challenging. Ted's favourite part was exploring the gorge at Hardraw, which provides a cooler, sheltered environment.

There is an entrance fee, paid at the Green Dragon, for the path to the waterfall (hardrawforce.com).

OS information

SD 875898
Explorer OL30

Distance
4.1 miles/6.6 km

Time
2¼ to 2¾ hours

Start/Finish
Hawes

Parking DL8 3NT
National Park car park, Hawes (pay and display)

Public toilets
In the car park

Cafés/pubs
Firebox Café, at start; White Hart Inn, Hawes; Green Dragon, Hardraw

Terrain
Lane and pavement; field paths and tracks; riverside path

Hilliness
Steep ascent 5 to 6 and descent from 7 to end

Footwear
Year round

Public transport

Bus service 113, between Gayle and Garside, to the Dales Countryside Museum stop at 🚶: littlewhitebus.co.uk

Accessibility

Suitable for powered wheelchairs between Hardraw 4 and Hardraw Force; generally suitable for all-terrain pushchairs, but these will need lifting over several stiles and narrow gates

Ted's tips

Keep on leads in all fields where there are livestock. Safe water entry points along the River Ure and the path to Hardraw Force from 4 is dog friendly. There are several narrow, gated stiles. At the Firebox Café there is outside seating; the White Hart Inn and Fountain Hotel are dog friendly; well-behaved dogs are also welcome at the Green Dragon

Scan Me

Did you know? The Dark Skies Festival in Hawes is part of the Yorkshire Dales National Park's International Dark Sky Reserves programme. Held every February, the festival features a variety of events including guided planet trails at the Dales Countryside Museum, stargazing sessions at the National Park Centre, and a rocket launch activity for families. Partakers can enjoy telescope viewings, nighttime photography, craft workshops, and nocturnal wildlife walks (darkskiesnationalparks.org.uk).

Local legend Hardraw Force, England's tallest single-drop waterfall, gained cinematic fame in *Robin Hood: Prince of Thieves* (1991), where it served as the backdrop for the scene in which Maid Marian discovers Robin Hood bathing beneath the falls. Set behind the Green Dragon inn, the dramatic limestone gorge has long inspired artists and poets, including JMW Turner and William Wordsworth.

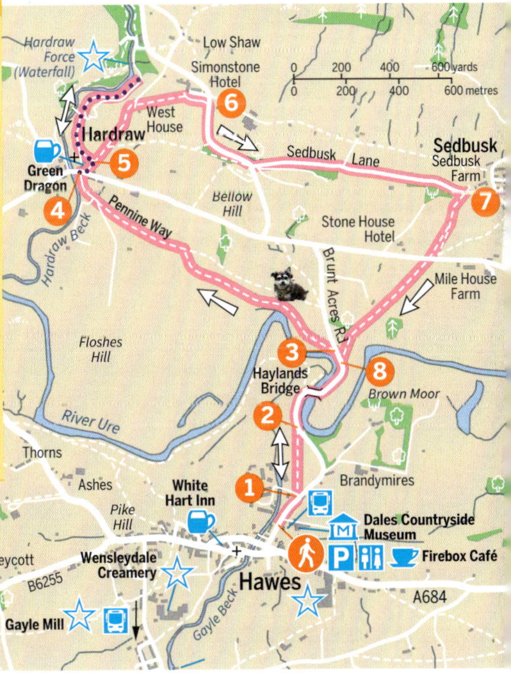

STORIES BEHIND THE WALK

☆ **Hawes** The town was granted its market charter in 1699, allowing it to hold weekly markets and annual fairs. This helped to transform the town into a thriving centre for trade in Upper Wensleydale. Farmers, craftsmen and merchants gathered to sell livestock, cheese and a wide variety of goods. This tradition continues today, the Tuesday market remaining a focal point, popular with locals and visitors.

☆ **Gayle Mill** Located in Gayle, just south of Hawes, the mill was built in 1784 as a water-powered cotton mill and is considered the oldest structurally unaltered mill of its kind in Britain. It later processed flax and wool before becoming a sawmill in the 1860s, powered by a rare Thomson turbine, still in use today. Following a major restoration in 2004, it reopened in 2008 as a heritage site. Visitors can now enjoy guided tours and demonstrations (gaylemill.org).

☆ Hawes
Dales Countryside Museum
Firebox Café

Gate onto Brunt Acres Road

Haylands Bridge (River Ure)

Set of gates

Pennine Way

½ mile

1 mile

National Park car park, Hawes

➡ Just beyond the toilet block, in the back-left corner of the car park, take the sloping path up to Brunt Acres Road.

➡ Turn **right**, cross to the opposite pavement and go over the old railway bridge, taking the first road turning, **left**.

1 ➡ Almost immediately, pass through a gate on the **right**, marked Pennine Way.

➡ Follow the flagged path across the pasture until you reach a gate, which leads back onto Brunt Acres Road.

V Wensleydale Creamery

The tradition of cheese-making in the area dates back to the 12th century when it was first established by Cistercian monks. The Wensleydale Creamery continues this legacy by using local milk and traditional production methods. Saved from closure in 1992 by local workers, it now thrives as both a visitor attraction and an award-winning artisan cheese producer (wensleydale.co.uk).

Dales Countryside Museum

Housed in the old Victorian railway station in Hawes, the Dales Countryside Museum tells the story of over 1,000 years of Yorkshire Dales life. Managed by the National Park Authority, it features indoor galleries and outdoor exhibits, including a steam locomotive and carriages. Interactive displays cover topics such as farming, mining, textiles, transportation and domestic life. With workshops, changing exhibitions, a café, a shop and accessible facilities, it offers a lively, educational experience for all ages (dalescountrysidemuseum.org.uk).

2 Bear **left** along the road, watching out for approaching traffic, for ¼ mile, crossing the River Ure and walking to a set of gates on the **left**.

3 Pass through the gate and set out in the fingerpost direction along the well-trodden field track to Hardraw, passing from pasture to pasture.

Continue as the path becomes flagged, the Pennine Way leading you through a gate onto the road at Hardraw, opposite the Green Dragon.

NATURE NOTES

The River Ure flows through Hawes with clear, fast-moving water, characteristic of upland limestone rivers. Brown trout and grayling thrive in its clean channels. Riverside trees such as alder and willow provide valuable cover for birds, while flower spikes of meadowsweet attract insects.

Each summer, the hay meadows display a vibrant array of flowers, including buttercups, daisies, clover, cranesbill and lady's mantle. Traditionally managed for hay, these species-rich fields can support up to 120 different plant varieties and attract essential pollinators like butterflies and hoverflies.

The beautiful, cascading song of the skylark may accompany you on the walk in spring and summer.

Hardraw Force is an impressive waterfall, with a dramatic single-fall drop of nearly 100 feet. Set within a limestone gorge, a short, wooded path leads to the viewing area. Along damp rock faces, ferns and mosses flourish, and birds such as dippers and wagtails are often seen. The waterfall is particularly striking after heavy rainfall.

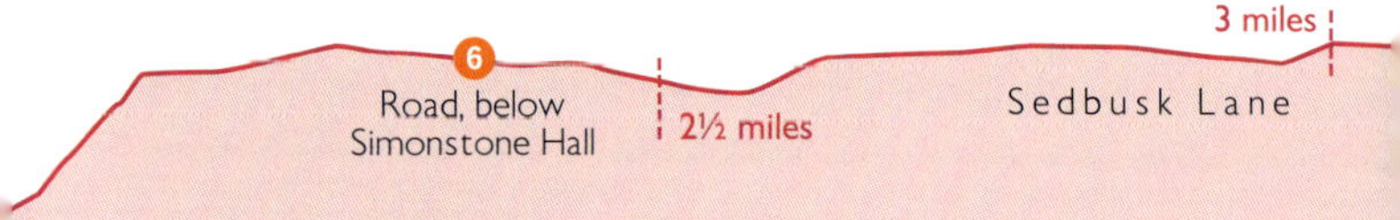

4 ➡ Turn **right** and then **left**, signed to the waterfall and pub car park. The entrance is accessed through the café for a small fee.

➡ There are two paths: the lower walk to the falls viewing area beside Hardraw Beck is accessible. Return to the pub.

5 ➡ At the pub's drive entrance, look **left** for a narrow gate, signposted Simonstone.

➡ Go through two gates on a short path by the side of a house.

➡ Begin climbing steeply up the field. Cross a stile by a millennium memorial and continue ascending until you reach outbuildings. Bear **right**, following the signs to Simonstone and Sedbusk, then pass below Simonstone Hall (left) and reach a road.

Above: wildflower meadow
Below: grey wagtail

Above: Hardraw Force
Below: lady's mantle

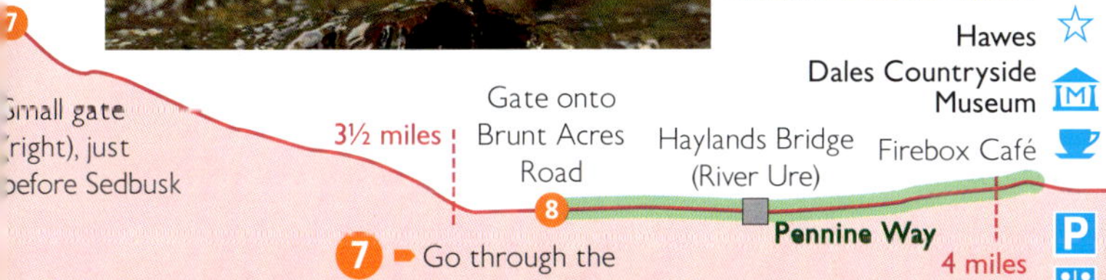

6 ➡ Turn **right** down the road, watching out for approaching traffic.
➡ Bear **left** at the junction with Sedbusk Lane (by a bench) and walk nearly ½ mile to a small gate on the right just before reaching the village.

7 ➡ Go through the gate and follow a field path down to a road.
➡ **Cross** the road to the gated stile and fingerpost (Haylands Bridge), opposite, and take the diagonal cross-field path, descending to a gate in a wall on Brunt Acres Road by the River Ure.

8 ➡ Go through the gate and turn **left** along the road, crossing the River Ure and retracing your outward route to the car park.

Opposite page (clockwise): peregrine falcon; sheep at Hawes; teasel
This page (clockwise): knapweed; buddleia; hazel catkins; badger

CATCH A BUS

WALK 5

KETTLEWELL TO BUCKDEN

This walk begins in Kettlewell, a village renowned for its charming stone cottages and picturesque network of small streams. The route to Buckden follows clear riverbank and meadow paths, with views of the surrounding fells, a variety of wildlife and heritage features typical of the Dales. The open ground and stream access make it ideal for dogs. Ted particularly enjoys the stretch near Starbotton, where the riverbank widens with plenty of splash-worthy spots that keep his tail wagging.

OS information

SD 967722
Explorer OL30

Distance
4.4 miles/7km

Time
2½ to 3 hours

Start Kettlewell
Finish Buckden

Parking
Yorkshire Dales National Park car park (pay and display)
Start BD23 5QZ Kettlewell
Finish BD23 5JA Buckden

Public toilets
In the car parks in Kettlewell and Buckden

Cafés/pubs
Kettlewell, Starbotton and Buckden

Terrain
Well-signed riverside paths, field paths and tracks

Hilliness
Almost flat

Footwear
Year round ; in dry conditions

Public transport
Bus service 72B, Buckden to Grassington: upperwharfedale.com

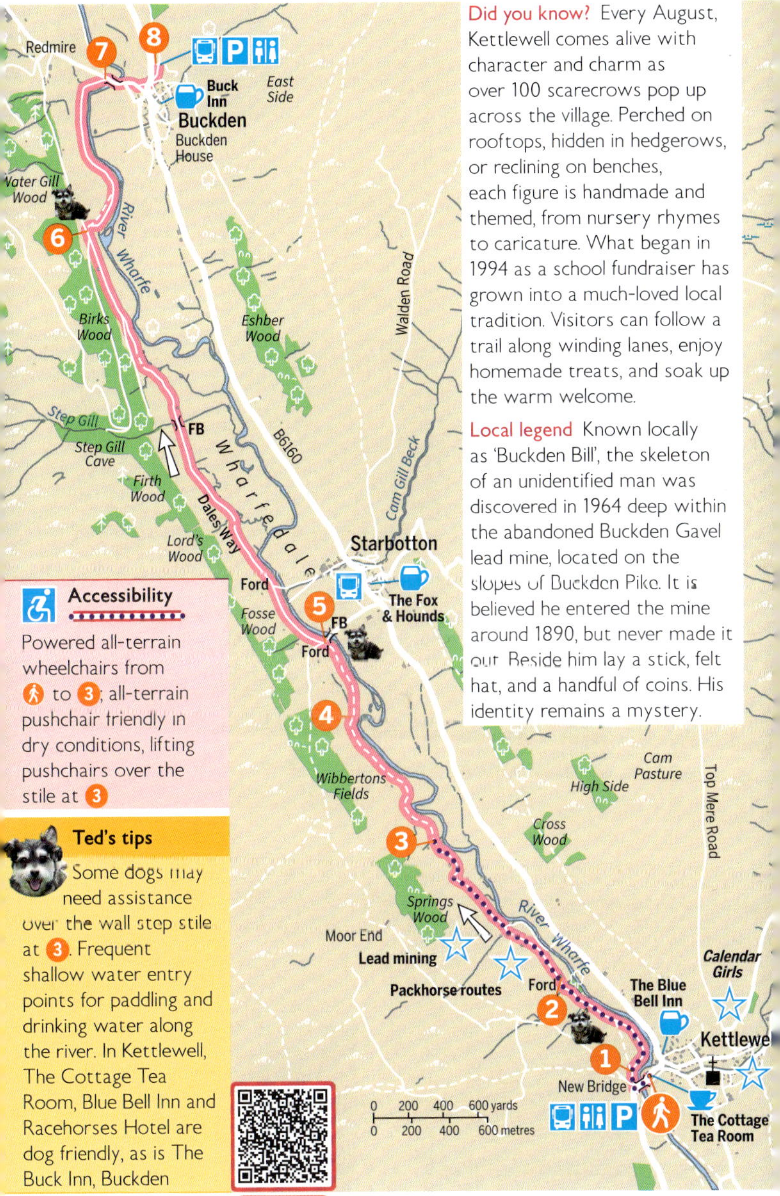

Did you know? Every August, Kettlewell comes alive with character and charm as over 100 scarecrows pop up across the village. Perched on rooftops, hidden in hedgerows, or reclining on benches, each figure is handmade and themed, from nursery rhymes to caricature. What began in 1994 as a school fundraiser has grown into a much-loved local tradition. Visitors can follow a trail along winding lanes, enjoy homemade treats, and soak up the warm welcome.

Local legend Known locally as 'Buckden Bill', the skeleton of an unidentified man was discovered in 1964 deep within the abandoned Buckden Gavel lead mine, located on the slopes of Buckden Pike. It is believed he entered the mine around 1890, but never made it out. Beside him lay a stick, felt hat, and a handful of coins. His identity remains a mystery.

Accessibility

Powered all-terrain wheelchairs from start to 3; all-terrain pushchair friendly in dry conditions, lifting pushchairs over the stile at 3

Ted's tips

Some dogs may need assistance over the wall step stile at 3. Frequent shallow water entry points for paddling and drinking water along the river. In Kettlewell, The Cottage Tea Room, Blue Bell Inn and Racehorses Hotel are dog friendly, as is The Buck Inn, Buckden

Scan Me

STORIES BEHIND THE WALK

☆ **Kettlewell** The village's origins date back to the early medieval period when Anglo-Saxon settlers established a community in Upper Wharfdale. The name derives from Old English 'Chetelewelle', meaning 'spring or stream of Chetel', which indicates a settlement around a natural water source. Initially a small farming hamlet, the Saxons cultivated crops and grazed livestock along the fertile valley. Their influence is evident through archaeological finds, field patterns and place names.

☆ **Lead mining** The history of Kettlewell and nearby Buckden has been greatly influenced by lead mining, which has left a lasting impact on the landscape of the Yorkshire Dales. Miners excavated deep shafts and tunnels, creating spoil heaps, hushes (channels carved to expose ore veins) and stone-built smelting mills. By the late 1800s, falling lead prices led to the closure of many mines resulting in abandoned workings, ruined buildings and a rich industrial heritage.

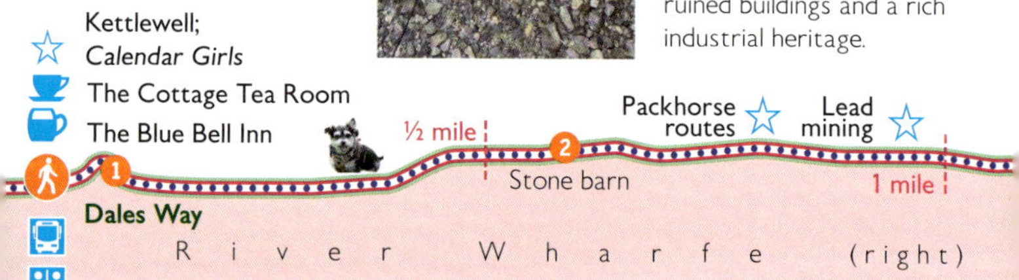

Yorkshire Dales National Park car park

➡ Leave the car park by turning **right** opposite The Cottage Tea Room and walking over the road bridge.
➡ Immediately after the bridge, go **right** again, keeping **right** to a gate.

1 ➡ Pass through the gate.
➡ Descend gently on the Dales Way and walk alongside the river to a stone barn in ½ mile.

☆ Packhorse routes

The villages of Kettlewell and Buckden thrived as vital staging points along ancient packhorse routes in Wharfdale. These rugged trails carried wood, lead and agricultural produce between remote Dales' villages and bustling towns. Stone bridges, inns and packhorse tracks remain visible, reflecting centuries of rural commerce and travel. Today, these historic paths offer walkers a glimpse into the challenging lives of the packhorse traders from those bygone days.

☆ *Calendar Girls*

Kettlewell gained fame as the fictional village of Knapely in the 2003 film *Calendar Girls*, starring Helen Mirren and Julie Walters. Filming took place around its iconic bridge, Middle Lane village hall, letter box, and Far Lane, featuring tai-chi scenes on the hillside. The village's timeless stone architecture and riverside charm helped craft the quaint, rural feel vital to the story.

2 ➡ Keep **ahead** on the gravel track, lined by drystone walls. ➡ Pass a barn over to the left, go through a couple of gates and reach a step stile built into a stone wall.

3 ➡ Once over the stile, the path opens up. Cross a small two-plank bridge over a beck and follow the well-trodden Dales Way across the fields to a gate.

NATURE NOTES

The hay meadows in Wharfedale burst into colour each summer. Managed for centuries through low-intensity farming, the meadows support a diverse array of wildflowers, including yellow rattle, eyebright, meadow buttercup, lady's bedstraw, ox-eye daisy and harebell. Common spotted orchids appear in sheltered areas. Cut late in the season and lightly grazed in the winter, the fields reflect a sustainable rhythm tied to the land.

Ringlets, meadow brown and marbled white butterflies drift low through the long grasses in summer, taking nectar from knapweed and field scabious. Small tortoiseshell and peacocks bask on stones or feed on thistles. Bumblebees, including red-tailed and buff-tailed varieties, are drawn to bird's-foot trefoil, clover and wild thyme.

The River Wharf meanders through the dale's hay meadows and alder-lined banks. Gravel shoals provide habitat for otters and spawning trout, while kingfishers nest in sandy banks. You can often see dippers and grey wagtails along the faster-flowing sections.

2½ miles

3 miles

River Wharfe (right)

4 Go through the gate, walk on and cross a wider plank bridge.

Continue across the fields, river to the right, through several more gates and wall gaps to a fingerpost and gate at a bridge across the Wharfe to Starbotton.

5 You can detour to the village, a five-minute walk, by crossing the bridge. (Fox & Hounds bus stop for the return to Kettlewell or on to Buckden.)

Otherwise, keep **straight on**. Follow the Dales Way across the meadows for 1½ miles to a fork.

Opposite page: kingfisher
Above: cranesbill and lady's bedstraw
Top right: ox-eye daisy
Bottom right: dipper

6 ➡ Bear **right** at the fork and continue on the Dales Way, passing from field to field, with the River Wharfe immediately on your right.

➡ In just over ½ mile, reach a wooden gate giving onto a lane.

7 ➡ Turn **right** onto the lane and **cross** the bridge, walking into Buckden.

➡ Keeping **left**, head up to the village green. Cross the road near the pub to the Dales National Park car park.

8 ➡ The bus back to Kettlewell departs from the bus stop by the car park.

WALK 6

CATCH A BUS

CLAPHAM AND INGLEBOROUGH CAVE

This beautifully scenic walk from Clapham to Ingleborough Cave is a gem for dog owners. The well-maintained route winds through woodland, limestone outcrops and beside a babbling beck, which are perfect for Ted's nose-led adventures. With gentle gradients, clear signage and shaded paths, it is ideal for families and accessible walking. Ted especially loves splashing in the beck and sniffing around the mossy walls.

OS information

SD 745692
Explorer OL2

Distance
3.2 miles/5.1km

Time
1¾ to 2¼ hours

Start/Finish
Clapham

Parking LA2 8EA
National Park car park, Clapham (pay and display)

Public toilets
In the car park

Cafés/pubs
The Old Sawmill Café; The Old Manor House; picnic benches at start and 7

Terrain
Village lanes and well-maintained track

Hilliness
Gently ascending to Ingleborough Cave and corresponding gentle descent to return

Footwear
Year round (keeping to the main trail)

Public transport Bus service 581, between Kirkby Lonsdale and Settle to the New Inn stop, Clapham, 150 yards south of : klch.co.uk

Accessibility
Suitable for powered wheelchairs and all-terrain pushchairs throughout (keeping to the main trail)

Ted's tips
Keep dogs on a lead. The main track is shaded by trees and there are plenty of splash spots along Clapham Beck. No stiles. The Old Sawmill Café has free treats and water bowls, and the Old Manor House pub is dog friendly too

Did you know? Clapham village is linked to one of Britain's most dramatic natural wonders, Gaping Gill. This vast underground chamber, into which Clapham Beck disappears, contains the tallest unbroken waterfall in England, plunging 320 feet into the cavern below. The beck's flow once powered a hydroelectric system installed in the 1890s by the Farrer family, making Clapham one of the first villages in the region to have electric lighting.

Local legend Clapham is associated with the eerie legend of Boggarts Roaring Holes, a series of limestone potholes located near Ingleborough. Folklore warns of a mischievous boggart, an invisible spirit believed to be responsible for missing items and eerie noises. Said to haunt the caves near Clapham, the boggart was feared for its pranks and occasional malevolence, especially after dark, when strange echoes stirred the imagination.

STORIES BEHIND THE WALK

St James Church Originally dating back to Norman times, St James's Church was initially dedicated to St Michael, with documents mentioning it as far back as 1160. The village and the church experienced damage during a Scottish raid following the Battle of Bannockburn in the early 14th century. The church tower dates from that time but much of the rest of the building is Victorian. The church used to be powered by the Ingleborough Estate's hydroelectric system, initially installed in the late 19th century.

Aunt Bessie's Grotto
A Victorian limestone folly, the grotto was built in the late 1800s by the Farrer family, who were influential landowners in Clapham, with their ancestral home at Ingleborough Hall. The grotto is named after Elizabeth Farrer, who enjoyed tea there with her footman. It offers scenic views of Thwaite Scars and was marked as a 'Station' on early maps. Today, it serves as a charming shelter for walkers.

National Park car park

The Old Manor House

St James Church

1 Hydroelectric power

The Old Sawmill Café

2

Path junction and information board

3

View across the Lake

½ mile

Money Tree

Rhododendron viewing area

➡ Walk to the car park entrance and turn **right** onto Church Avenue, in the Ingleborough Cave direction, and continue to St James Church.

1 ➡ The route follows the lane round to the **left** (the Ingleborough Estate Nature Trail is to the right).
➡ Continue past the church, go **right** at the T-junction along Riverside to The Old Sawmill Café, noting the waterfall (right).

☆ **Hydroelectric ower** The Ingleborough state features a historic ydroelectric system, installed iitially to power Ingleborough Iall. A generator powered by vater turbine is found at the orth end of the village by the vaterfall. Fed by a diverted tream, the system reflects arly innovation in renewable nergy, and generated lectricity for the church and treet lighting in the village. The Old Sawmill Café has a further urbine as an exhibit.

☆ Ingleborough Cave

Although the cave entrance was well known, the vast underground chamber beyond was only discovered in 1837 by Victorian explorers who broke down cave walls and drained a subterranean lake to reveal the cavern. Visitors can follow a well-lit path past stalactites, flowstones and formations such as the Witch's Fingers and the Gothic Arch. One of Yorkshire's great natural wonders, the cave offers family-friendly adventure through 450 million years of geological history (ingleboroughcave.co.uk).

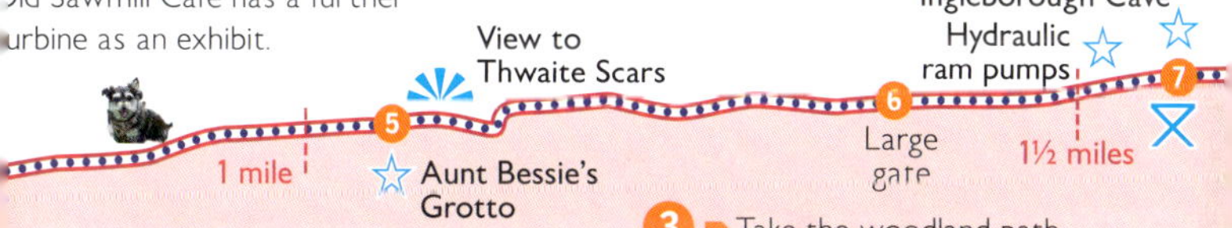

2 ➡ Enter the café to pay the walk entrance fee (there's a further fee for the caves). If the café is closed, use the pay machine at the main entrance.
➡ From the café proceed along a surfaced path and onto the track to reach a signposted junction and information board.

3 ➡ Take the woodland path to the **right**. There are directional arrows along the route. The lake appears, right, as the track widens.
➡ Pass a lake information board and then the 'Money Tree'.
➡ The track ascends gently to the rhododendron viewing area, right.

NATURE NOTES

Common hedgerow species found along the route include hawthorn, blackthorn – noted for its sloes in late summer – hazel and dog rose, with the hedges managed through traditional laying techniques. Mature ash and sycamore trees are recurrent in field corners and along the neighbouring Ingleborough Estate paths. Small coppices of oak and birch are found along Clapham Beck. These provide habitat connectivity for a range of woodland-edge wildlife, with the brimstone and speckled wood butterflies taking full advantage.

Clapham Beck flows through the village before joining the River Wenning, downstream. The beck supports aquatic life including in the slower-flowing vegetated pools, common frogs. Kingfishers are occasionally seen along the beck, especially near overhanging bankside vegetation where they hunt small fish. The watercourse is fed by springs and surface runoff from Ingleborough, which helps maintain good oxygen levels. Shaded areas and gravel beds provide suitable habitats for spawning and feeding for fish and amphibians.

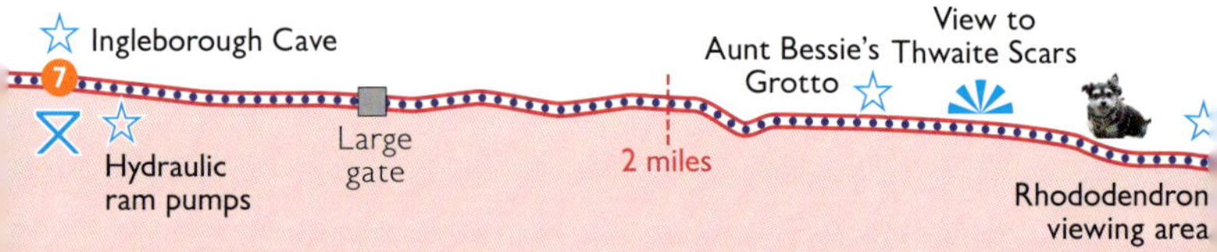

4 ➡ Shortly after the bench and information board, the path bears **left**.
➡ Carry on to Aunt Bessie's Grotto.

5 ➡ At the grotto there are good views of Thwaite Scars.
➡ After passing the grotto, continue along the woodland walk until you reach a large gate, which leads to Ingleborough Cave.

Above: hawthorn
Below: blackthorn

Top: dog rose
Bottom: peacock

Money Tree

View across the Lake

2½ miles

Path junction and information board

The Old Sawmill Café

Hydroelectric power

St James Church

3 miles

The Old Manor House

National Park car park

6 ➨ Go through the gate. As the path widens, you will see the beck to your right and Thwaite Scars, beyond. Notice the hydraulic ram pumps by the side of the beck – you can often hear them too.

➨ Keep **straight on** to the cave entrance and picnic area.

7 ➨ There is a fee to enter the caves, they are partly accessible, and dogs are welcome inside but strictly on leads.

➨ Simply retrace your outward route and return along the main track, enjoying the views from the opposite direction.

WALK 7

SETTLE AND GIGGLESWICK

This charming circular walk offers a gentle mix of town heritage, riverside scenery and village character. It passes landmarks like Victoria Hall and Settle Railway Station, follows the tranquil River Ribble, and explores the quiet stone-lined streets in Giggleswick. The terrain is mostly level and ideal for relaxed walking. Ted particularly enjoys sniffing along the grassy riverbank, pausing in shady spots, and trotting happily along the quiet lanes.

OS information

SD 816636
Explorer OL41

Distance
2.2 miles/3.6km

Time
1¼ to 1¾ hours

Start/Finish
Kirkgate, Settle

Parking BD24 9DZ
Ashfield car park (pay and display)

Public toilets
Whitefriars car park, BD24 9JD

Cafés/pubs
The Wonky Cake Café; The Golden Lion; Settle

Terrain
Lane and pavement; surfaced pathways

Hilliness
Mostly flat, with a moderate ascent to Giggleswick, 4 to 5, and corresponding descent, 5 to 6

Footwear
Year round

Public transport
National rail services to Settle Station, 150 yards south of start: nationalrail.co.uk
Bus services 580, from Skipton, and 581, from Kirkby Lonsdale, to the Market Place stop on Church Street, 150 yards from start: kirkbylonsdalecoachhire.co.uk

Accessibility

Suitable for powered wheelchair and all-terrain pushchairs throughout

Ted's tips

Keep on leads. Off-lead sections are further upriver, off this route. Water is available at the Wonky Cake Café. No stiles or livestock, but take care about the town

Did you know? The Settle Flowerpot Festival takes place each summer from mid-July to early September, transforming the town into an open-air gallery of imaginative displays crafted from recycled flowerpots. Residents, schools and businesses contribute hundreds of creations, ranging from cartoon characters to historical figures, positioned throughout the streets, shopfronts and hidden corners around the town. Trail maps guide visitors around the installations, encouraging exploration beyond the Market Place.

Local legend Opened in 1853 as the 'Settle Music Hall', Victoria Hall on Kirkgate holds the remarkable distinction of being the oldest surviving music hall in the world. Initially created by Reverend James Robinson to bring culture and education to the community, it has hosted a wide range of public events, from operatic performances and concerts to lectures. It remains a well-used venue and a rare surviving link to Settle's early dedication to the arts.

STORIES BEHIND THE WALK

☆ **Settle** The town began as an Anglian settlement in the seventh century and appears in the Domesday Book of 1086. Granted a market charter in 1249, it thrived through the wool and leather trades, later expanding with the development of 18th-century turnpikes, textile mills and the arrival of the railway in 1847. Its growth from a medieval market centre to an industrious Victorian town reflects Settle's adaptability and strategic location, foundations that still support a vibrant community of independent shops, weekly markets and cultural events.

Giggleswick School Chapel Crowned by its striking copper dome, Giggleswick School Chapel was built between 1897 and 1901 to mark Queen Victoria's Diamond Jubilee. The Grade II-listed building blends Gothic architecture with Mediterranean influence, and its richly decorated interior features mosaics, marble flooring and bronze statues. The dome, once used by wartime pilots for navigation, remains a landmark in the Dales.

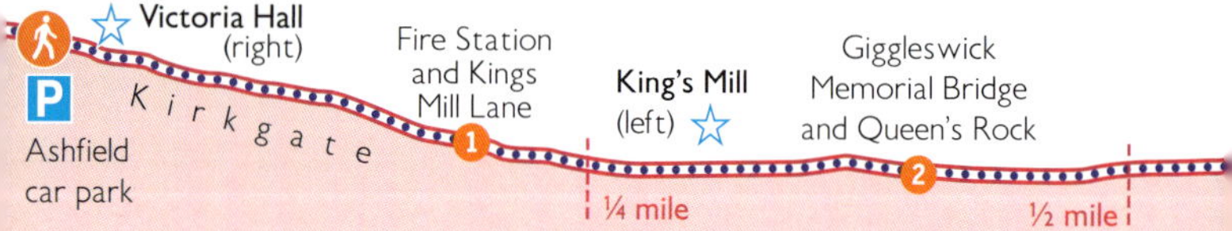

➨ In the car park, with your back to Settle Bowling Club, walk **forward** to Kirkgate.
➨ Turn **left** along Kirkgate, passing Victoria Hall (right).
➨ Keep **ahead** under the railway bridge and proceed along Kirkgate to the fire station on the corner of Kings Mill Lane.

1 ➨ Turn **left** to follow Kings Mill Lane past a garden centre (left) to the blue fingerpost where the path narrows.
➨ Continue on Kings Mill Lane, bearing **right** and then **left** to reach Giggleswick Memorial Bridge and Queen's Rock.

☆ **King's Mill** Built around 1830 by John Procter, King's Mill was originally operated as a cotton mill. It later served as a snuff mill and eventually as a paper store, before being converted into residential flats. The four-storey building features cast-iron columns and a bolted queen-post roof, with a late 19th-century extension. Procter also built cottages for the labour force nearby, known as Procter's Row.

☆ Settle Station Water Tower

Erected in 1876, Settle Station Water Tower is a rare survivor of the steam age and it once served as one of eight watering points for locomotives on the Settle–Carlisle line. Holding 43,000 gallons, it supplied engines tackling the steep 'Long Drag' northbound. Horses were stabled beneath the tank, and its robust cast-iron structure remains intact. Restored in 2011 and featured on Channel 4's *Restoration Man* series, it now serves as a private residence while preserving the town's railway heritage.

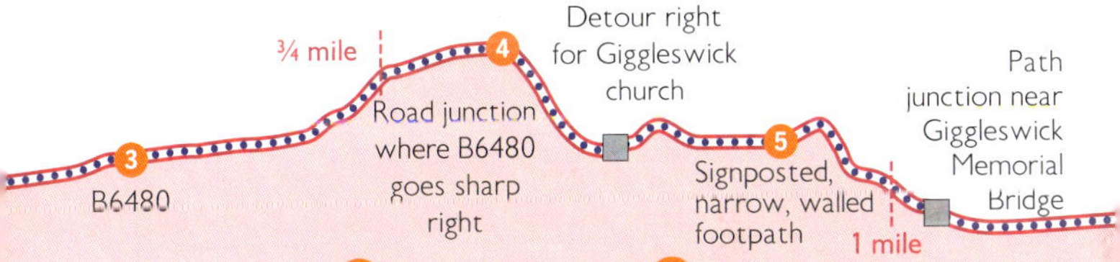

2 ➡ **Cross** the bridge, turn **right** at the signpost and follow the riverside path until you reach the main road, B6480.

3 ➡ At the main road, turn **left** (the bridge over the River Ribble, right) and follow the leafy pavement uphill until you reach an intersection in Giggleswick village where the B6480 goes sharp right.

4 ➡ Fork **left** into the village down Belle Hill.

➡ At the T-junction, detour **right** to visit the church.

➡ Otherwise, go **left** onto Bankwell Road. Walk to a path turning on the left.

NATURE NOTES

The River Ribble flows through the heart of Settle and supports a diverse range of flora and fauna. Atlantic salmon spawn in the upper reaches of the river. Purple-loosestrife is a striking, tall plant found on the riverbanks near the water's edge, with vivid magenta flower spikes that bloom from June to September. Along the path verges, look out for greater burdock whose Velcro-like burs can easily get caught on clothing and your dog's coat. Despite its name, leaves of red dead-nettle do not sting and can flower from March through to October. Brimstone and orange-tip butterflies drink nectar from spring flowers along the riverbank pathway.

Peregrine falcons are often seen above Castleberg Crag, the limestone outcrop that towers over Settle to the east of the town, where they have occasionally nested on the sheer cliff face. Their high-speed swoops are a thrilling sight. Along the Ribble's wooded banks, redstarts arrive in the spring, with the males flashing their distinctive bright, rust-coloured tails, favouring old stone walls and hollow trees for nesting.

Purple-loosestrife

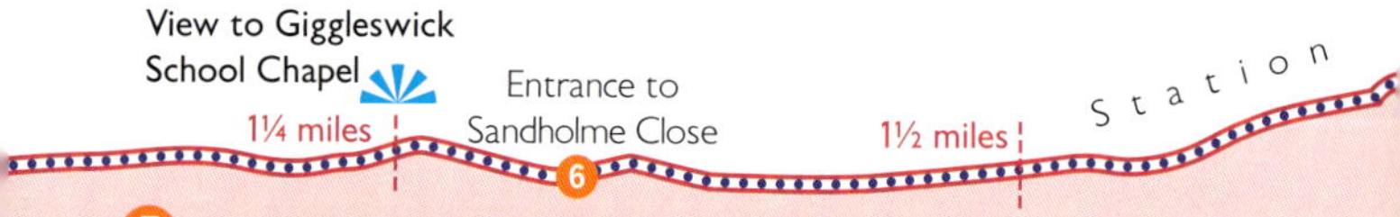

5 ➡ Go **left** along the footpath, bending **left** near the end to emerge at a path junction by the bridge **2**.
➡ Turn **right** and follow the riverside path, signed Railway Station, to Sandholme Close, at the end of playing fields (right).

6 ➡ Keep **ahead** along Sandholme Close to Station Road and go **left**.
➡ Follow Station Road for nearly ½ mile, crossing over the River Ribble, until you reach the railway station by an unusual water tower.

Top left: common redstart
Above: red dead-nettle
Bottom left: greater burdock
Below: peregrine falcon

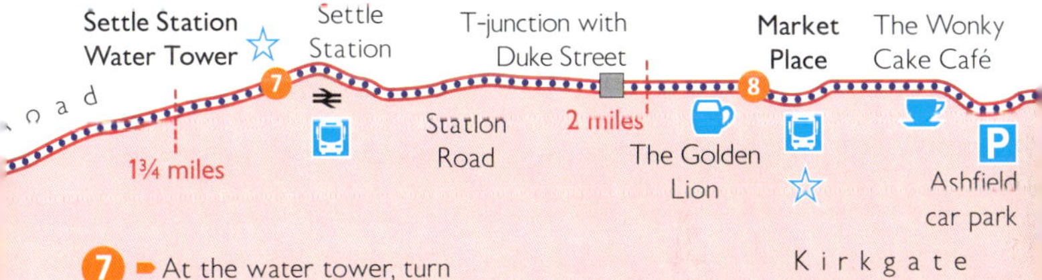

7 ➡ At the water tower, turn **right** for a closer look and to explore the old station.
➡ Resume the walk by continuing along Station Road to the T-junction with Duke Street.
➡ Turn **left** along Duke Street to the crossroads with Cheapside and Kirkgate.

8 ➡ The Market Place is **ahead** on the right.
➡ Turn **left** onto Kirkgate and pass The Wonky Cake Café (dog-friendly) on Bishops Court, or return to the car park.

Opposite page (clockwise): Redmire Village Pub; Wharfe View Tea Room, Burnsall; The Cottage Tea Room, Kettlewell
This page (clockwise): Hawes Ice Cream Parlour; The Blue Bell Inn, Kettlewell; Easby Loop Café, Easby; Kibble Bakery Coffee House, Skipton; The Old Sawmill Café, Clapham

BOLTON ARMS

THE
EASBY
LOOP
CAFE

BURNSALL ICE CREAM
WharfeView
Tea Room

THE
COTTAGE
TEA ROOM

WALK 8

GRIMWITH RESERVOIR

Set amid expansive moorland and big skies, this reservoir circuit combines easy terrain with rich upland scenery. The well-maintained path skirts water, reeds and rough grassland, with plenty of room to roam. Wildlife sightings, from waders to wildflowers, add seasonal interest. Dogs are welcome: Ted loves racing the wind and rooting in the rushy corners near the shore – a peaceful loop for families, nature watchers and energetic paws.

OS information

SE 063640
Explorer OL2

Distance
4.3 miles/7km

Time
2½ to 3 hours

Start/Finish
Grimwith Reservoir

Parking BD23 5ED
Yorkshire Water's Grimwith Reservoir car park

Public toilets
In the car park

Cafés/pubs
Picnic benches and seasonal ice cream van at start; Time Café at Stump Cross Caverns, on the B6265, 3.4 miles east of start

Terrain
Firm, compacted-surface paths; grassy paths; some uneven ground

Hilliness
Gently undulating, with a slightly steeper descent 1 to 2 and a short rise back to the car park

Footwear
Year round in dry conditions; after wet weather

Did you know? The Yorkshire Dales Sailing Club is located on the reservoir's southern shore, not far from the car park. Recently, the Royal Yachting Association officially recognised the club as a training centre and a British Sailing Pathway Club. A variety of sailing and windsurfing activities take place, with classes available for a range of abilities, as well as canoeing, kayaking and paddleboarding (yorkshiredales.sc).

Local legend Some say Grimwith means 'ghost wood', and it is easy to see why. On misty days, the reservoir and surrounding moor can feel quiet and eerie. Trees and drystone walls can seem to appear out of nowhere, and walkers have talked about strange silences or feeling watched. The landscape definitely has a way of stirring the imagination.

Public transport

Limited, seasonal, Sunday and Bank Holiday service 822, between Pocklington and Grassington, stops at the Yorkshire Water access drive entrance on the B6265, 1 mile south-west of 🚶: dalesbus.org

Accessibility

Suitable for robust, powered wheelchairs and all-terrain pushchairs throughout

Ted's tips

Welcome but keep on leads where there is grazing livestock and as directed by seasonal ground-nesting bird signs. No stiles. No swimming or paddling due to the deep water. Ted loves the wind-blown grass and puddle hopping

Scan Me

STORIES BEHIND THE WALK

☆ **Drystone walls** The drystone walls surrounding Grimwith Reservoir reflect historic field boundaries established long before the reservoir's construction. Made without mortar, these walls are built with carefully placed local gritstone, using traditional techniques adapted to harsh upland conditions. Some walls delineate former farmsteads, such as Gate Up, whil[e] others mark grazing enclosures. Their varied heights and width[s] indicate differing agricultural uses. Today, these ancient features also serve as a wildlife corridors and nesting sites for birds.

☆ **Lead mining** The moorland surrounding Grimwith Reservoir shows substantial evidence of historic lead mining, dating from the 18th and early 19th centuries. You can still see waste stone spoil heaps, where miners once sorted ore by hand. Old mine shafts are also scattered across the area, now sealed off for safety. Much of this activity was run by local estates, including the Duke of Devonshire's. The Dales landscape here was shaped by industry, long before the reservoir existed.

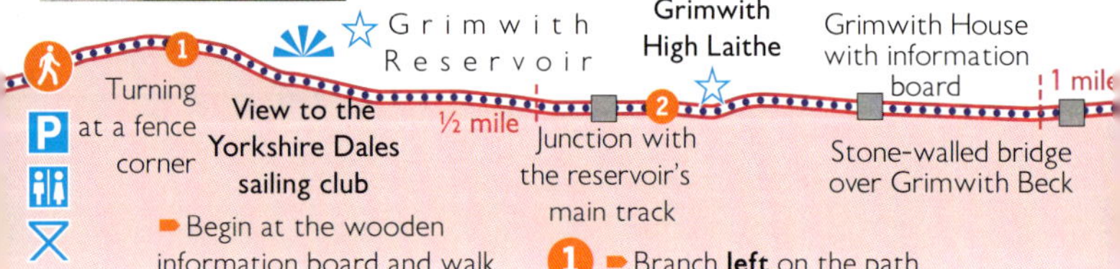

➨ Begin at the wooden information board and walk across the car park to a fingerpost signed Round the Reservoir.

➨ Proceed along the surfaced track to a path leaving on the left at a fence corner in 200 yards.

1 ➨ Branch **left** on the path, descending gently across the grassy slope (view, left, to the sailing club). Rejoin the main surfaced track at the eastern end of the reservoir.

➨ Go **left** towards the thatched barn ahead.

☆ Grimwith Reservoir

Dating from the 1860s, Grimwith Reservoir was constructed to supply water to Bradford's growing population during the Industrial Revolution. Located in the uplands of the Yorkshire Dales, it remains the largest reservoir owned by Yorkshire Water. Over time, it has developed ecological importance, supporting bird species such as curlew and oystercatcher. The surrounding landscape includes blanket bog and acid grassland. Today, the site also serves as a recreational centre, for sailing, walking and nature watching (yorkshirewater.com).

Farmhouse ruin and moorland; drystone walls

1½ miles ☆ 3 2 miles

☆ Grimwith Reservoir

☆ Grimwith High Laithe

The rare 16th-century cruck-framed tithe barn passed near 2 was carefully dismantled and rebuilt in the 1980s when the reservoir was expanded, saving it from submersion. Its sweeping oak beams and timeworn stone give a feel for how Dales' farm buildings once looked and worked: sturdy, simple and built to last. You get a real sense of past rural life just standing beside it at this quiet, photogenic spot.

NATURE NOTES

Curlews nest in the rough pasture and boggy ground north and west of the reservoir, their distinctive call heard across the moor. Lapwings prefer open fields near the eastern end of the walk. Redshanks favour the wetter margins near Blea Gill.

The moorland surrounding the reservoir is characteristic of the Dales uplands, dominated by heather and bilberry. Managed through controlled burning and grazing, it supports bird species like red grouse and short-eared owls.

Between Blea Gill and Gate Up Gill, you can find wet ground that supports bog asphodel, which grows here from late spring, with small yellow flowers that prefer open, marshy areas. In summer, meadowsweet and banks of rosebay willowherb line the path to High Laithe and orchids grow around the barn.

The damp and sheltered conditions around peripheral shallow pools and slow-moving inlets provide breeding grounds for common frogs, smooth newts and, occasionally, toads. In warmer months, dragonflies and damselflies patrol the water's edge, particularly near reeds and sedges along the gills.

Rosebay willowherb

Grimwith Reservoir

2 ➡ After visiting the barn – Grimwith High Laithe – continue on the main track, anticlockwise around the reservoir, for 1 mile. You'll pass Grimwith House (information board), cross a stone-walled bridge and reach a ruin (information board) on the north side of the reservoir.

3 ➡ Continue along the shore track as the path narrows. ➡ Soon pass through a gate, walking for ⅔ mile to a bridge over Gate Up Gill.

Top left: curlew
Bottom left: short-eared owl
Above: lapwing
Below: bog asphodel

3½ miles

Gate leading onto a grassy strip at the western end of the reservoir dam

Reservoir valve tower

4 miles

Grimwith Reservoir

Gate onto the reservoir access drive

Yorkshire Water's Grimwith Reservoir car park

4 ➡ **Cross** the bridge, and then another over Blea Beck in the reservoir's north-west corner.

➡ Bend **left** with the track, following it to a turning on the left in ½ mile, looking down on a barn.

5 ➡ Turn **left**, downhill, bending **right** beyond the barn. Carry on to reach a gate.

➡ Go through the gate, following a wall (left) on a grassy strip that soon crosses the reservoir dam. Pass the valve tower and come to a gate.

6 ➡ Pass through the gate and turn **left** along the dam's access drive.

➡ At the next junction, keep **right** and return to the car park.

WALK 9

BURNSALL

This beautifully scenic walk takes you through one of the Dales' most charming villages. Situated in the heart of Wharfedale, this circuit features tranquil riverside paths, wildflower meadows and gentle climbs, offering sweeping views of limestone scars and some fascinating historic architecture. Ted particularly loves splashing in the shallow waters and exploring the dry-stone walls for interesting scents. The mix of open fields and shaded paths should suit most dogs.

OS information
SE 031611
Explorer OL2

Distance
2.5 miles/4km

Time
1½ to 2 hours

Start/Finish
Burnsall

Parking BD23 6BS
Burnsall car park (pay and display)

Public toilets
In the car park

Cafés/pubs
Riverbank Café at start; Wharfe View Tea Room and Red Lion Hotel, Burnsall

Terrain
Lanes; firm, grassy field and riverside paths; steep steps down from Burnsall Bridge

Hilliness
One moderate climb after leaving Burnsall

Footwear
Year round (trainers) in dry conditions; (boots) after wet weather

Public transport
Bus services 74, Dales Bus, between Ilkley and Grassington, and 74A, between Hebden and Ilkley, to the Burnsall Bridge stop, near start: transdevbus.co.uk/coastliner; northyorks.gov.uk

Accessibility

Suitable for wheelchairs from (start) to 1 and 6 to end; all-terrain pushchairs throughout but with steps after (start) and narrow suspension footbridge at 5

Ted's tips

Keep on leads where there are livestock and along the lanes. No stiles but a flight of steps after (start). Shallow-water entry points for paddling and drinking after 5 at Sandbed Beck

Did you know? St Wilfrid's Church features an unusual octagonal clock, one with the earliest pendulum and iron workings in an English church. Installed in the late 17th century, its extended pendulum reflects remarkable early engineering, likely the result of a skilled local craftsman, though the creator remains unknown. Today it is maintained by electronic windings, quietly marking time above the green.

Local legend Though sightings are rare, a ghostly figure is reputed to cross Burnsall's packhorse bridge at dusk, a lone walker with a gaunt face wearing a dark wide-brimmed hat. Said to appear without warning, he vanishes just as quickly. Some claim he is Thomas Denholme, a former villager with unfinished business, and the tale has lingered in local folklore for years.

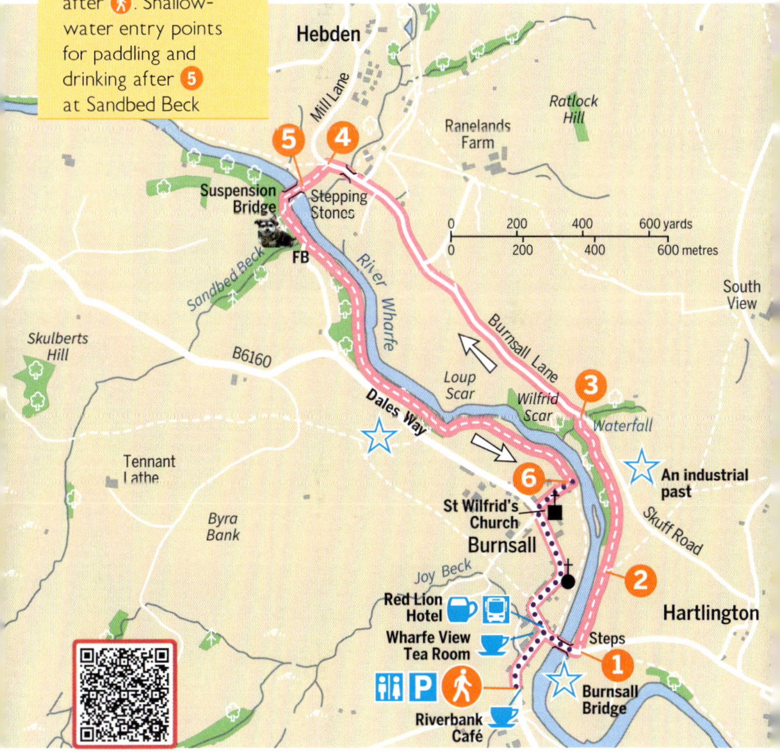

Scan Me

STORIES BEHIND THE WALK

☆ **An industrial past** The industry here may have been small scale, but it played a key role in daily life. Spinning and weaving were common in cottages and barns, with some still retaining large upstairs windows for letting in light. The River Wharfe powered mills, including a fulling mill near the village. Outbuildings near the green suggest trades like blacksmithing and tanning. The village's industrial heritage lives on in its buildings and layout.

☆ **Dales Way** Burnsall lies along a historic packhorse route that once carried goods like wool, lead and salt between market towns and monastic centres, including Bolton Abbey and Grassington. The Dales Way now follows parts of these paths. While the original surfaces are mostly lost, the route towards Appletreewick shows signs of sunken lanes, deepened by centuries of traffic. Stone stiles, gateposts with worn grooves and enclosed farm tracks are all still visible.

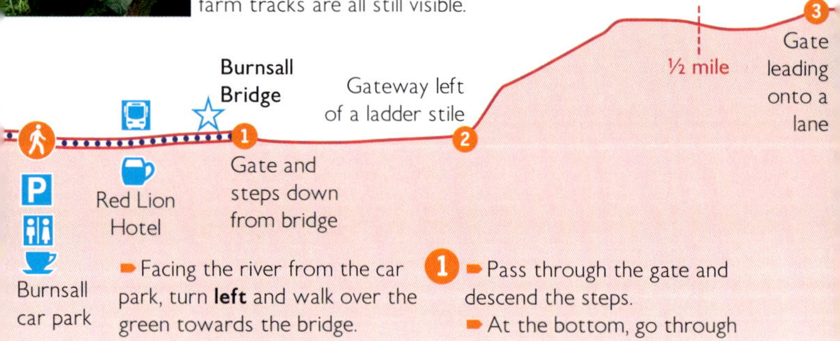

➡ Facing the river from the car park, turn **left** and walk over the green towards the bridge.

➡ In front of the Red Lion Hotel, turn **right** across the bridge to reach a gate on the **left**.

1 ➡ Pass through the gate and descend the steps.

➡ At the bottom, go through the double set of gates and follow the riverside path across the field to a gateway by the river to the left of a ladder stile.

☆ Burnsall Bridge

Burnsall Bridge is one of the most beautiful gritstone bridges in the Yorkshire Dales. Built in the early 1600s, the village has records of crossings here dating back to the 14th century. Initially designed for packhorses and carts, it replaced timber structures that were swept away by floods. Its five low arches curve gracefully over the River Wharfe. Today, the bridge accommodates the B6160 and is a picturesque focus for walkers through the village.

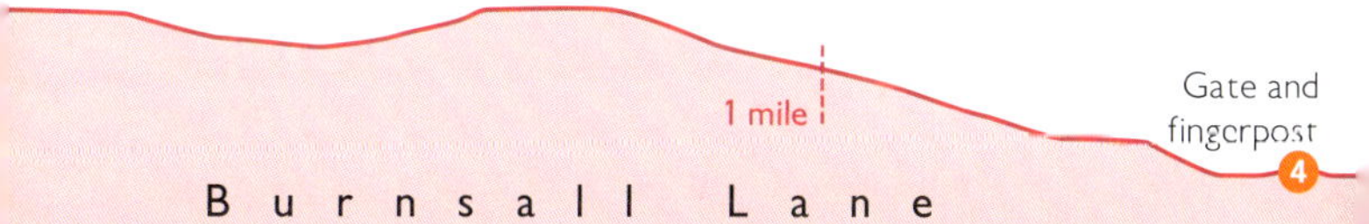

St Wilfrid's Church

A Grade I-listed building, St Wilfrid's has origins stretching back to Saxon times. Rebuilt in stone after the Norman Conquest, it now blends medieval, Tudor and Victorian features. Highlights include a circular Norman font, a 14th-century alabaster Nativity panel, and Anglo-Scandinavian stone carvings. Viking tombstones found nearby suggest an early settlement. The lychgate is one of the few in Yorkshire with counterbalanced weights.

NATURE NOTES

Insect-attracting knapweed blooms in summer along the banks of the River Wharfe. Known for its creamy-white flowers in spring and purple-black berries in late summer, the elder is a common hedgerow tree.

Herons may be seen near the suspension bridge at 3 and downstream towards Lowbank's Plantation, where quiet pools offer favourable hunting grounds.

Trout are resident year-round, favouring shaded pools and fast-flowing sections of the river. Atlantic salmon pass through in autumn, as they head upstream to spawn. The depth, flow conditions and clean water over the gravels near Burnsall Bridge are suitable for spawning activity.

Swaledale sheep are a regular sight in the fields around Wharfedale. With their curled horns and distinctive faces, they are a fitting emblem of the Yorkshire Dales National Park.

Damp stone walls and shaded rocks host lichens, ferns and insects, forming rich microhabitats along the Dales Way. Near the churchyard, look for hart's-tongue fern and common polypody growing in crevices beside mosses and crustose lichen.

Common polypody

2 ➨ Pass through the gateway and begin a short climb, rising on the field path to the trees ahead.

➨ Go through a gate on your **left** onto a woodland path, which winds for 375 yards to a narrow gate leading onto a lane.

3 ➨ Turn **left** and walk along the lane, heading towards the parish of Hebden.

➨ On reaching the village outskirts in ⅔ mile, cross a stream and look out for a fingerpost and gate on the **left**.

4 ➨ Pass through the gate and walk down the grassy path towards the river, going through a gate in an intermediate wall before reaching a suspension footbridge.

Left: Ted looking for ducks **Right**: heron

Left: hart's-tongue fern
Middle: thistle
Right: elderberries

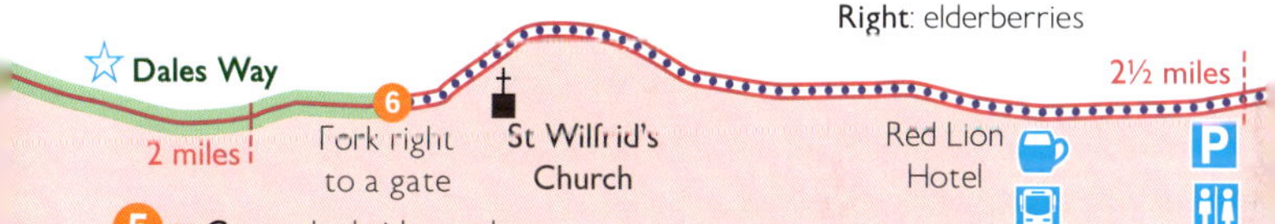

5 ➡ **Cross** the bridge and turn **left** onto the riverside path (Dales Way).

➡ Keep beside the river for ¾ mile, heading back to Burnsall.

➡ Approach the village and watch for a path fork. Bear **right** on the narrower path and head up to a gate.

6 ➡ Go through the gate along the surfaced lane, which runs between a row of cottages and the church.

➡ Turn **left** at the end onto the pavement of the village road (B6160) and follow it back to the village green and return to the car park.

WALK 10

SKIPTON CASTLE WOODS

This lovely walk follows woodland paths beside Eller Beck. Starting near the Old Saw Mill, it skirts Skipton Castle's medieval walls and meanders through mature trees and coppiced glades. Dogs will enjoy varied terrain, shaded trails and safe splash access. Before or after your walk, explore the cobbled streets, canalside paths and dog-friendly spots in town. Ted's paws-down favourite stretch is along the River Valley route, where he can explore safely on his extendable lead.

OS information

SD 993521
Explorer OL2

Distance
1.9 miles/3.1km

Time
1¼ to 1¾ hours

Start/Finish
The Bailey, Skipton

Parking BD23 1UA
The Bailey car park (charge)

Public toilets
High Street car park, Skipton, BD23 1ED

Cafés/pubs
Kibble Bakery Coffee House, Sheep Street; The Castle Inn, Mill Bridge, near 1; Skipton

Terrain
Pavement and tarmac path; firm, crushed-stone path on the River Valley Route 3 to 5; woodland path, muddy after wet weather

Hilliness
Gentle descent to 1; very gradual ascent from 1 to 5

Footwear
Year round in dry conditions; after wet weather 5 to 6

Public transport

National rail services to Skipton; the station is 0.9 mile south-west of (start): nationalrail.co.uk Bus services to The Bailey stop at (start) – 14, Skipton and Embsay circular: northyorks.gov.uk/public-transport and 64 and 873, Ilkley to Skipton: transdevbus.co.uk/the-keighley-bus-company

Accessibility

Suitable for powered wheelchairs from the Old Sawmill entrance at 3 as far as 5, returning by the same route; all-terrain pushchairs throughout, but note steps at 2 and 5

Ted's tips

Keep on leads in town and on leads or under close control in Skipton Castle Woods. The waterway banks can be steep in places. No stiles

Did you know? Skipton has long been a traditional market town, but in the 19th century it was also a thriving textile-manufacturing hub, especially cotton spinning and weaving, with mills like Belle Vue and High Corn Mill employing many local people.

Local legend During the English Civil War, Skipton Castle faced persistent cannon fire. To soften the blows, defenders hung sheep fleeces over the walls, an ingenious tactic that helped preserve the fortress. Legend has it that the wool absorbed the impact and saved the castle from ruin. The tale lives on in Skipton's coat of arms, where the fleeces represent resilience, resourcefulness, and the stubborn spirit of a town that refused to fall.

STORIES BEHIND THE WALK

Skipton Castle The Castle was constructed around 1090 by Robert de Romille, a Norman baron. Its strategic location guarded the gateway to Wharfedale. The castle remained a military stronghold until the 17th century and famously withstood a three-year siege during the English Civil War. The castle's medieval glory was restored in 1659 by Lady Anne Clifford. Features include a twin-towered gatehouse, banqueting hall and a chapel. Today, it is one of England's best-preserved medieval castles open to the public.

Medieval hunting grounds Skipton Castle's medieval hunting grounds once covered the area now known as Skipton Castle Woods. These woodlands served as a vital resource for the castle's residents, supplying timber, firewood and wild game. Noblemen hunted deer, boar and game birds within the managed forest. Evidence of medieval woodland management, including coppicing and boundary earthworks, can still be traced.

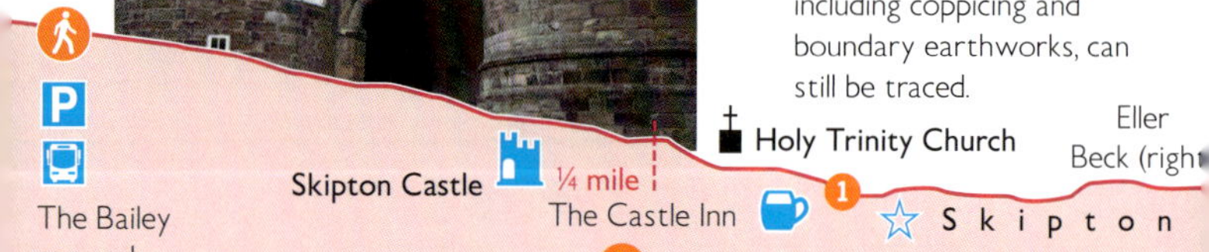

From the bottom end of the car park, follow The Bailey path, bending **right** and then passing the castle entrance, Holy Trinity Church and The Castle Inn, keeping **ahead** to Mill Bridge. There's a seating area, either side of which are steps and a ramp.

1 **Descend** from the bridge.

Keep **forward** along the path by the side of the old mill building, past a water wheel (left).

Continue along the walkway to its end, a stone wall to your right, until you reach a small metal footbridge.

Town Hall

Built in 1862 on the site of a former vicarage, Skipton Town Hall became the civic heart of the town in 1895, replacing the old hall on Sheep Street. Its proportions and detailing are typical of mid-Victorian civic buildings. Over time it hosted council meetings, concerts and community events. Today, it houses the Craven Museum, which includes Roman finds and local artefacts. A 2021 restoration introduced accessible facilities, gallery space and improved public access.

Skipton's old deer park Once part of the castle's medieval deer park, Park Hill is situated adjacent to Skipton Castle Woods. For centuries, it served as pastureland and estate grounds, and evidence of ridge and furrow agriculture can still be seen today. In the 19th century, areas of the park were adapted for quarrying and farming. Although it is now mostly private land, the parkland retains some of its feudal character, featuring mature trees, drystone walls and views over the town.

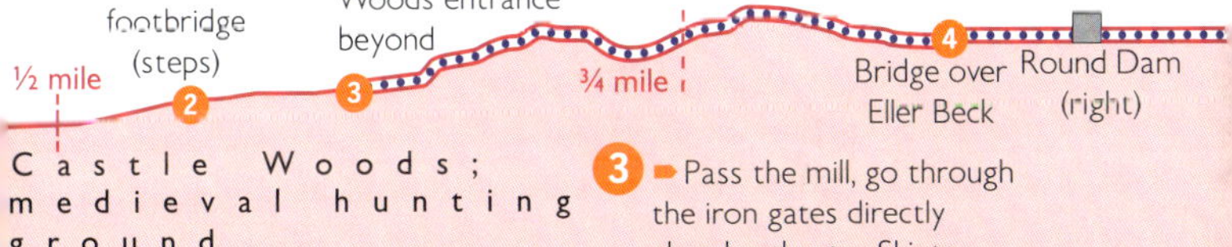

2 Cross over the footbridge, go up the steps at the other side, and follow the surfaced path round to the Old Sawmill entrance. (Note the date on the wall plaque, 1785.)

3 Pass the mill, go through the iron gates directly ahead and enter Skipton Castle Woods.

Proceed through the woods, Eller Beck to the right, for ¼ mile to a bridge. Look out for the Spirit of the Medieval Huntress sculpture on the way.

NATURE NOTES

Skipton Castle Wood's ancient woodland comprises mixed broadleaved tree species such as ash, oak, hornbeam and sweet chestnut. On the River Valley Route, alder can be seen along the riverbanks. In spring, catkins of both sexes are borne on the same tree, the male ones being distinctly longer than the females.

Carpets of dog's mercury and wild garlic (ramsons) cover the woodland floor before the tree canopy comes into full leaf.

Go quietly and you may be lucky enough to spot a roe deer, while the woodland is also home to badgers and five species of bat. If you visit late on a summer evening you have a chance of spotting brown long-eared, common pipistrelle, Daubenton's, Natterer's and noctule bats.

The drumming of great spotted woodpeckers may be heard in the woods, but these shy birds are more difficult to spot. Keep a lookout above the trees for buzzards and red kites, the latter distinguished by their forked tails.

Dog's mercury

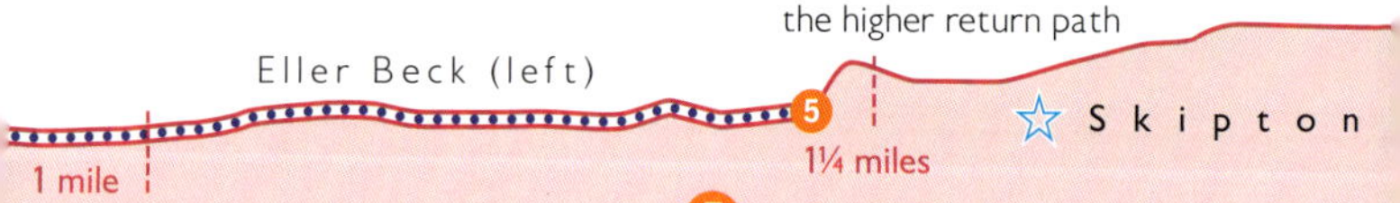

4 ➡ **Cross** over the bridge and immediately bear **left** to Round Dam lake.

➡ Walk past the lake (right) and continue with Eller Beck (left) for ¼ mile to a path junction and flight of steps, right, and a road bridge ahead.

5 ➡ Turn **right** and climb the steps. At the top, turn **right** again and return on the higher path.

➡ Keep the drystone wall to your left, pass the steps down to Round Dam, and carry on for ⅓ mile, beside the wall, to a Skipton Castle Woods gate.

Top left: great spotted woodpecker
Above: badger
Left: red kite
Below: commom pipistrelle

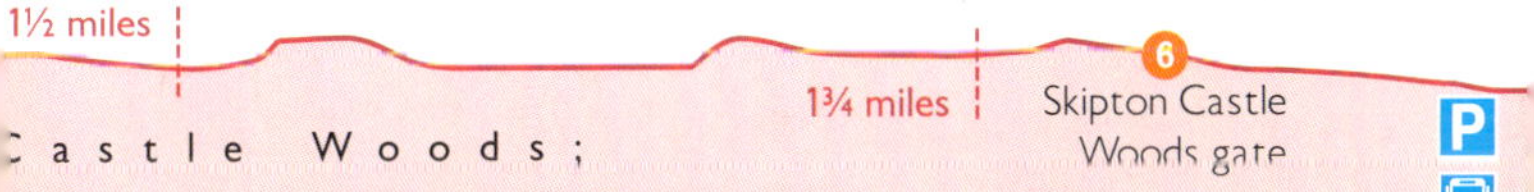

Castle Woods; medieval hunting ground

6 ➡ Pass through the iron gate and turn **right**.
➡ Very shortly, turn **right** into the car park to conclude the walk.
➡ To visit the castle, church or explore the town, retrace your steps on The Bailey path.

Ted inside Kibble Bakery Coffee House

Ordnance Survey

Publishing information

ISBN 978 0 319093 07 8
1st edition published by Ordnance Survey 2026.
Batch Number: 02/26–1

ordnancesurvey.co.uk

While every care has been taken to ensure the accuracy of the route directions, the publishers cannot accept responsibility for errors or omissions, or for changes in details given. The countryside is not static: hedges and fences can be removed, stiles can be replaced by gates, field boundaries can alter, footpaths can be rerouted and changes in ownership can result in the closure or diversion of some concessionary paths. Also, paths that are easy and pleasant for walking in fine conditions may become slippery, muddy and difficult in wet weather.

If you find an inaccuracy in either the text or maps, please contact Ordnance Survey at os.uk/contact.

A catalogue record for this book is available from the British Library.

General Product Safety Regulations (GPSR) Visit quicklinks.osmaps.com/gpsr for information on compliance, safety and recalls.

Milestone Publishing credits

Author: Sally Outram

Series editor: Kevin Freeborn

Maps: Cosmographics

Design and Production: Patrick Dawson, Milestone Publishing

Printed in Great Britain by Pureprint

Photography credits

Front and back cover: Sally Outram.

All photographs supplied by the author Sally Outram except page 6 Emily Gill (Ordnance Survey); 18, 33 Kevin Freeborn.

The following images were supplied by **Alamy Stock Photo**: page 5, 74 malcolm stoney; 23 John Morrison; 30 Robert Lazenby; 36 Gareth Dobson; 51 tim gartside; 65 Ian Lamond.

The following images were supplied by **Shutterstock.com**: page 19 Gabriela Beres; 24 Sunbunny Studio; 25 jamie corney; 25 kacege; 39 bieszczady_wildlife; 40 Lewisjnewman; 41 Henk Bogaard; 46 HTU; 47 WildMedia; 73 Marco Bongera; 73 Martin Fowler; 79 Luka Hercigonja; 79 Erni; 79 Lewisjnewman.

The following images were supplied under **CC BY-SA 2.0**, via Wikimedia Commons: page 19 John Poyser; 25 Alan Hughes; 30 Gordon Hatton; 31 Anthony Harrison; 33 Peter Trimming; 33 DS Pugh; 41 Derek Harper; 45 Steve Partridge; 53 Anne Burgess; 58 gail hampshire; 59 Evelyn Simak; 67 Mike Pennington; 71 Colin Smith. The following image was supplied under **CC BY-SA 3.0**, via Wikimedia Commons: 32 DDd; 53 Charles J. Sharp; 59 Jerzy Strzelecki; 67 Alpsdake; 67 Hajotthu; 72 Carolina Latorre Canet; 78 Aroche; 79 Barracuda1983.
The following image was supplied under **CC BY-SA 4.0**, via Wikimedia Commons: page 19, 67 Charles J. Sharp; 25 Philip Halling; 39 Gerda Arendt; 59 Robert Flogaus-Faust; 59 Vladimir Kharuk.